EXPLORING THE BIBLE

EXPLORING THE BIBLE

A Survey of the Holy Scriptures

by

KENDIG BRUBAKER CULLY

MOREHOUSE-BARLOW CO.

NEW YORK

Course 9 Reader

Printed in the United States of America

6-98765

TO THE STUDENT

FOR SOME YEARS now, you probably have attended Church
School classes in your home parish wherever you have lived.
You have learned many things about the Christian religion.
Your studies have helped you grow more familiar with the
life and practices of the Church; given you some deeper
awareness as to why being a Christian makes a big difference
in your life; introduced you more intelligently to the reasons
for the ways in which we worship God. Also, we are sure
that you have heard a great deal about the Holy Bible and
have learned quite a few things about various parts of it.

During the present year you are going to share with the
others in your group in a deeper exploration of the Bible.
Up until now you have probably only looked into the Bible
in a kind of piecemeal way—here a little, there a little—but
the time has now come when you doubtless want to take a
fuller look at the Bible as a whole. What, really, are these
writings about which we hear so much in the Church? How
shall we tell the difference between Genesis and Revelation
(the first and last books in our Bible)? What kinds of writings
do we have here? What is the purpose of the different writers?

The fact is that every Christian needs to know the Bible
well enough to find God's Word in and through its writings,
both for himself and for the whole Christian community.
Just as no one could possibly understand Shakespeare's real
message in one of his great plays unless he actually saw the
play presented in a theatre or read it in a book, so, surely,

5

no one can understand what the Bible is really saying unless he studies it carefully and over a period of time really becomes able to find his way around the book.

We shall have several aims, therefore, as we go into this study together. We hope that you will come to see the full sweep of the contents of the Bible. We hope that you will learn to find your way around in the Bible so that it will become like a genuine friend to whom you often turn for inspiration and help. We want you to have the joy that uncounted millions of people before you have known in getting acquainted with a book that is more than any other book because it is *the* Book of Life.

Don't expect too much of one year's study. Obviously you can't expect to learn everything that is in the Bible and back of it, just through studying this one course. Some of the world's greatest scholars have spent lifetimes studying the Bible without being able to know all about it. We don't want to be like the young girl who went into a bookstore and asked for a book that would tell her *all* about penguins, for she came back later and complained that the book told her more than she needed or wanted to know about them! The Bible is not a book that you can master all at once—not even in a year's time. It is a book for your lifetime's study. Now, however, is a good time to start looking at it as a whole, so that you can learn how to be at home with it whenever you meet it in church or by yourself.

KENDIG BRUBAKER CULLY

CONTENTS

7

8 CONTENTS

LIST OF MAPS

The following maps will be found in the colored insert in the center of the book.

Part I
THE LAW

1

ONE BOOK

IF YOU LOOK at the Table of Contents of a copy of the Bible, you will note that there are two big sections. First is the Old Testament. Under "Old Testament" you will find listed thirty-nine titles. Then comes the New Testament with twenty-seven titles. (In some Bibles you will find an extra section called the Apocrypha, inserted between the Old and New Testaments.) If you add these two together, you will see quickly that the Bible contains sixty-six separate writings. It looks as if we have here a whole library of books rather than merely one book, and that is exactly right, for each of these books arose out of a particular situation and was put together by one or more different writers.

Why, then, you ask, are they bound together as one book? To answer this question would take a whole book itself, but we can state briefly the reason. The people of God cherished each of these writings separately because all of them grew out of the religious experience of the Hebrew-Christian tradition. Every single book in the Bible was written by someone who was interpreting what God said to the people who were involved in some particular situation. All the books put together came to be precious to these people because in them as a whole God's dealings with His people could be clearly seen. This is what we mean when we call the Bible the "Holy Scriptures." They do not merely list facts as do some history text books. These writings tell of God's dealings with men and women and men's and women's response to God's action;

13

they are writings of faith. In them, God's mighty acts for our salvation are set forth, and for this reason they occupy a very special place in the life of the Christian Church.

The Collect for the Second Sunday in Advent in the Book of Common Prayer expresses the way in which Christians approach the Scriptures:

> Blessed Lord, who hast caused all holy Scriptures to be written for our learning; Grant that we may in such wise hear them, read, mark, learn, and inwardly digest them, that by patience and comfort of thy holy Word, we may embrace, and ever hold fast, the blessed hope of everlasting life, which thou hast given us in our Saviour Jesus Christ. *Amen.*

The Word of God guides us to discover in these ancient writings the way of life for ourselves in this, our present time of history. They tell of things that happened a long time ago, but those are things which through faith are important for us today, just as they will be equally important for our descendants for all the years to come.

The word *Bible* in English is a translation of a Greek word which means *The Books.* When we add *Holy* to the title, we are saying what these books mean to us, for God has had a hand in them and they are holy because He speaks to us through them in the Church.

Two Big Sections

The writings of the Old Testament were produced in the time of the people called Hebrews, whose history spanned long centuries. They lived from roughly two thousand years before Christ, and their descendants are the modern-day Jews. The actual writing of the historical books in our Old Testament was done by editors in about the sixth century B.C., but some parts of the books are much older, stretching way back to the time when stories were told by word of mouth from parents to their children before anything was written down in permanent form on scrolls.

The New Testament contains writings that grew out of the life of the Early Christian Church, the oldest parts being the letters of St. Paul, which were written during the middle of the first century A.D.

The Jewish people share the Old Testament with the Christians. They refer to the Bible, just as we do, but by this they mean only the Old Testament books, and these are placed somewhat differently from their location in the Bible as we have it. The old Jewish classification of the books of the Old Testament is still a useful one. In the chapters to follow we shall discuss these books under three types: the Law, the Prophets, and the Writings. For us it is important to realize that our Lord, Jesus Christ, was familiar with the Scriptures of the Hebrew Bible, which He probably studied very much as we study the Bible today in Church School. However, He knew the Scriptures much more thoroughly than most of us ever do!

When the writings which make up the New Testament were finally put together by the Early Church, they were referred to as the New Testament because the Christians regarded Jesus as the new act of God to bring salvation to all mankind. The Hebrew religion was regarded as part of God's revelation to man—an absolutely necessary part. Because they found a new Word of God given them in Jesus Christ, they tended now to think of Him as the dividing-line of history. From now on Christians would refer to B.C. (Before Christ) and A.D. (Anno Domini, the Year of the Lord). The Old Testament tells the history of God and His people before Christ; the New Testament tells the continuing history after Christ. The word *Testament* means *Covenant*—a relationship that God offers which is accepted in faith and obedience by His people, who respond to Him.

Thus we can say that the Bible is one book, even though it has two big sections, and even though each of those two sections is in turn made up of numerous smaller writings. The whole Bible refers to one continuing action of God and one continuing stream of response to God on the part of His people. We cannot really understand all that Jesus Christ means to us as Lord and Saviour except against the background of God's dealings with the Hebrews in all the centuries B.C. Christians also believe that one cannot really understand the Old Testament, either, except as it is seen as the long preparation of the people of God to receive the Light of the World which came through Jesus.

Several Things to Remember

So, as we begin this study, it is important for us to remember several things about the Bible:

(1) It is a very old book. It wasn't produced by a single writer who sat down one day to write a book that he hoped would be a best-seller. Long before anything was written down, people had certain experiences with God, and even these were not written in final form, in most cases, all at one time. As we mentioned before, things were told by word of mouth long before they were recorded on scrolls. Then, too, editors would often work over the scrolls, making copies and changing statements to fit their purposes in writing. Sometimes we see how this editing process resulted in the inclusion of several different versions of the same material within the Bible; for example, the Ten Commandments are stated somewhat differently in two places—Exodus 20 and Deuteronomy 5.

(2) It is a book about God, first of all. It is literature, of course; or, we could say more truly that it *contains* very fine

literature. As we shall see, there are all kinds of writing here: history, poetry, laws, drama, sermons, and so on. For the Christian, the Bible is much more than mere literature: it is a book whose message comes home to us only when we read it in faith.

(3) It is a book shared by the people of faith who are members of the whole Christian Church. This is why we do not only read the Bible as individuals, but we hear it read in the worship of the Church; we study it together in the Church; and our clergy teach us in their sermons what the Bible says to us in our need and for our living. As individuals, of course, we should read the Bible, but even when we do so in the quietness of our own rooms, we are surrounded by a great cloud of witnesses—those in all generations who have found in this ancient book the living Word of God.

2

HOW THE OLD TESTAMENT
WAS WRITTEN

IT MAY BE a surprise to you to learn that the order in which the books are placed in the Bible is not the order in which they were written.

Actually, most of the books of the Bible represent the weaving together of various strands of writing by editors. This is especially true of the Old Testament. The very oldest pieces of writing in the Old Testament, in fact, are not whole books at all, but little sections that were later incorporated by the editors into the final documents. Examples of these are the Song of Miriam in Exodus 15:21 and the Song of Deborah in Judges 5. In Exodus, Miriam, who was the sister of Moses and Aaron, lifted a tambourine in her hand after the Hebrews had crossed the Red Sea. She sang, while the women danced to the music:

> Sing to the Lord, for he has triumphed gloriously; the horse and his rider he has thrown into the sea.

The reference is to the drowning of the Egyptian horsemen in the water as they tried to pursue the escaped Hebrews. In Judges, Deborah's song celebrates the victory of the Hebrews over the Canaanites, whose general, named Sisera, came to an inglorious end in the battle near Megiddo.

Even some of the writings that obviously are the work chiefly of one writer (such as some of the prophets' books,

18

which we shall be looking at later) show marks of having had a number of hands involved in the way in which they were finally put together.

The first five books of the Old Testament, often referred to as the Pentateuch (the Five Scrolls), illustrate this clearly. The scholars have shown how in these books several sources have been put together. These have been given special names: J, so called because it prefers the name Jahweh, or Yahweh, for God; E, which uses the name Elohim, another Hebrew word for God; D, which is mostly the book of Deuteronomy; and P, which re-works the material from the standpoint of the priests of Israel. Each of these strands comes from a different geographical location and time. We have no need to go into all of this in detail, for it is a highly complicated matter mostly of interest to scholars. The way in which the material was put together until it reached final form around 400 B.C. is a fascinating story.

The Oral Tradition

Back of the literary (written) forms, as we have said, there lay long centuries of the telling of stories by word of mouth. The time during which the Old Testament history was taking place, we must remember, is very ancient (two thousand years before Christ down to the time of Christ; in other words, as long ago as four thousand years before our own time). Writing materials were scarce. We know that important records were kept by the Egyptians and Babylonians on stone monuments and clay tablets. Imagine the labor involved in recording even the important public happenings of last year, let's say, on tablets of stone, and that without even the instruments such as a modern cemetery monument dealer has available to inscribe a few names and dates! The process of writing things down on scrolls was also quite complicated. For one thing, papyrus was scarce. Oftentimes practical considerations determined the very length of a book. Some Old Testament writings are only as long as there would have been room on the single scrolls originally used for writing them down.

The result was that the Oriental peoples depended largely on unwritten tradition for the passing down of information from generation to generation. Stories of the patriarchs (Abraham, Isaac, Jacob), bits of history, poems and ballads (like Miriam's and Deborah's), and so on, became part of the lore of the people. This still happens in families sometimes, as you can realize when you think of some older person's recounting events of the past which were not of course important enough for anyone to write down, but which had real interest to members of the family involved. The difference in the case of the Hebrews was that the great events remembered were deeply bound up with their common religious history. The great leaders of their past, from Abraham on, had become a part of their tradition; and events like the Exodus could never be forgotten because it was through such men and such events, they felt, God had been leading His chosen people. Eventually, these things were written down, both so as to be better remembered and to assure that oncoming generations would not forget either.

The Hebrew Bible

In the Hebrew Bible the books eventually were gathered together into three sections. The first five books were called Torah (the Law). Although we tend to think of books like Joshua, Judges, I and II Samuel, I and II Kings as history, the Hebrew Bible called those writings "the Former Prophets." Isaiah, Jeremiah, and Ezekiel, along with The Twelve (whom we call minor prophets—Hosea, Joel, Amos, Obadiah, Jonah, Micah, Nahum, Habakkuk, Zephaniah, Haggai, Zechariah, and Malachi), were called "the Latter Prophets."

The other writings were called exactly that, "The Writings," and included Psalms, Job, Proverbs, Ruth, Song of Songs, Ecclesiastes, Lamentations, Esther, Daniel, Ezra-Nehemiah (treated as one book), and I and II Chronicles (also one book). Why were the historical books called "prophets"? It was thought that these histories were written by persons called prophets, men who not only told about history but interpreted it. The Hebrews thought of history as being governed by a divine purpose, and they were never interested in facts merely for the sake of facts. They thought of any happening in history as an event in which God was doing something or saying something to His people.

Language

The theological seminary where your parish priest studied doubtless teaches courses in Hebrew. Not all candidates for the Episcopal Church's ministry are required to study Hebrew, although they must be examined in New Testament Greek, unless excused by the Bishop. Many men do study Hebrew, however, for that is the language in which the Old Testament books were written. It is no longer a "dead language," if, indeed, it *ever* was, for today Hebrew is again a spoken language being used in the modern state of Israel, in the common everyday speech of the people as well as in the religious services and theatre.

Hebrew is a language belonging to a group of languages sometimes called *Semitic*. Another of these ancient languages was Aramaic, which by the time of Christ had become the ordinary speech of the people. The rise of Greece under Alexander the Great led to the wide use of Greek throughout the ancient world, and it was then that the Hebrew Bible was translated into Greek. That translation is called the Septuagint (which means "translated by seventy men"). When the Christian Church spread outside Palestine into Asia

Minor, the Septuagint (Greek) Bible was used, for the Gentile (non-Jewish) Christians did not know the Hebrew language. Thus the Hebrew Bible continued to be the Bible of the early Christians until their own writings were collected into the New Testament, at which time the Hebrew Bible became the "Old Testament" for the Church.

3

CREATION AND FALL

Now WE ARE GOING to go into a study of the biblical books themselves, and the best way in which to do this will be to keep your Bible handy as you read the chapters in this book. It will not be expected that you will read every single word in every book at this time, but certainly there would be no point in studying the Bible if all we did were to read *about* the Bible, especially since copies of the Bible are readily at hand so that everyone can own his personal copy. For ease in reading, it is suggested that you use the Revised Standard Version. This is the latest widely-used version available, combining as it does the beauty of language of the Authorized Version (King James)—the one most frequently used in our Church's worship—and the freshness of style that modern people enjoy reading.

For today's portion look up Genesis 1, 2, 3, and 4, the chapters that tell of the early Hebrews' conception of the beginning of the world and of mankind. If you have never read this material before, you will certainly enjoy getting firsthand the biblical account of how the world was created and how man was put on earth. These stories date back to very early times, and are so old that no one could possibly point to their origin. Primitive peoples had always had their myths in which they tried to answer the question "Why?" in relation to the wonderful, mysterious world in which they found themselves living. Man seems to *have* to explore that question. No group of people anywhere has ever been content, as far as we know, merely to accept what is, without trying to find the reason for it all.

Throughout the ancient world various peoples came up with their differing explanations of how things started, yet there is a similarity at points between the myths of surrounding Near Eastern nations and those of the Hebrews. The difference between them is that the Hebrews' account attributed the origin of all things to God alone. There were other gods worshipped by the nations who were their neighbors, but always the Hebrews insisted that only Yahweh, the true God, deserved man's worship. Notice the first of the Ten Commandments: "You shall have no other gods before me" (Exodus 20:3). God Himself was not created by anything or anyone else. He Himself always was, always will be, and to Him alone can be attributed the cause of all else that came into existence. Hence He alone is worthy to receive worship.

In this early story we can see the origin of the Sabbath day, the seventh day of the week. It is said that God rested on the seventh day from His work of creating—and for that reason the day was hallowed, that is, set apart as a day of rest. The Sabbath continued as the holy day of the Jews, as indeed it does even today. Christians, after the Resurrection of our Lord, which occurred on the first day of the week, chose to observe Sunday instead of Saturday as the special day of worship in the week.

Paradise

The world was made by God, but for a purpose involving man, according to Genesis. It was to become the dwelling place of a creature whom God wanted to put into the world so that He might show His love for that creature and receive the creature's love in return. In other words, God introduced man into the world He had made. The Genesis account gives the famous paradise story. This is the Garden of Eden narrative, about which almost everyone knows whether he has read it for himself or not. We can see here how the old account gives answers to many questions—why sex? why pain? why the necessity to work? The basic question has to do with the problem as to why man refused to recognize God and sought instead to follow his own desires and will. When Adam and Eve ate the fruit of the forbidden tree, they were, in effect, saying to God that they knew as much as He, and this pride became the basic sin of man for all the years to come. This is what we have heard theologians call *original sin*. It is interesting to note that the word *Adam* means, in Hebrew, *man*. This story is not just referring to the first man and woman, Adam and Eve, as individual persons, as if they were John and Josephine. It is referring to the way man himself really is in his inner being: wanting to assert himself against God, wanting to put himself in place of God.

Cain and Abel

The struggle between Cain and Abel is told in Chapter 4 of Genesis. Back of this story is an important aspect of the Hebrews' life. You will notice that when the two brothers offered their sacrifices to God, Abel's was accepted, but Cain's was rejected. What did each of the brothers bring as his offering? Cain had become a tiller of the soil, a farmer, and he brought the fruit he had raised. Abel, apparently, instead of settling down as a farmer in one place, continued to be a shepherd—that is, he followed the herds. His offering was a newborn animal, "the firstlings of his flock and of their fat portions" (Genesis 4:4). It is thought by many scholars that this story reflects a deep-seated struggle among the early Hebrews. Many preferred to settle down in the towns and establish farms to be passed from generation to generation, whereas others preferred to continue the old nomadic way of life that had characterized the children of Israel up to the time of their settling in the land of Canaan.

The important thing about the Cain and Abel story, however, with its brutal murder and Cain's question, "Am I my brother's keeper?" (Genesis 4:9), is this: it shows that already in the history of the race of man, things go wrong because man is sinning instead of living closely to God. This breaking up of man's peace and harmony is shown even more strongly in the Noah story that follows, as well as in the Tower of Babel incident. Instead of paradise, man by his choices had brought great evils into his life through his wanting to be independent of the God who had created him.

What about These Myths?

These stories of beginnings raise some interesting questions in our minds.

For one thing, they make us ask, What kind of material is this? How shall we regard these stories? It is important for us to recognize that these are not like the history or science that we study in school. Remember what we said earlier about the Bible as a book of faith. It is when we read these stories from the standpoint of trust in God that we can best find out what they are saying. They are not trying to give a scientific account of the origin of the world. They were written long before the rise of modern science, with all that geology, astronomy, physics, and chemistry can tell us about the way in which the earth may have unfolded. Nor are these accounts of history written as are the accounts of the origin of the United States of America in terms of the facts about the first settlers and the development of the original Thirteen Colonies. After all, no eyewitnesses sat around making notes as to how Cain and Abel acted toward each other or how Noah and his family rode out the flood in their ark. No reporters were able to take tape-recordings of conversations to report in the local newspaper! These accounts are true in a religious sense—for they state in story form truths that are always true: God makes and sustains His world; when men and women co-operate with Him, they can know His love and give love to Him; when men and women turn their backs to God or seek to make themselves the center rather than God, their lives become all mixed up.

4

A CHOSEN PEOPLE

FROM GENESIS 11:26 through Chapter 36 we continue the look backward to the early days of the Hebrews, whose history is seen here through the eyes of the first fathers of Israel, the Patriarchs—Abraham, Isaac, and Jacob. The compiler of Genesis very skillfully links this story of the historical beginnings of Israel with the other stories of the beginnings of the world and the first inhabitants. The earliest chapters deal with history that can be said to belong to everybody, but with the Patriarchs we start reading the history that is a particular and special history, that of the Hebrew people themselves. Yet you will note in Genesis 11:10–24 there is a family tree, a genealogy, tracing the line of descent from Shem, a son of Noah, to Terah, the father of Abraham. This means that the writer wanted to connect Israel's historical beginnings with the earliest stories that had come down out of the past. All history is seen as one, in other words. What God intended from the creation of the world He now proceeds to carry out through the destinies of this one people, Israel.

Abraham is regarded in the biblical story as the very father of the Israelite people. In the Hebrew language, the name *Abraham* signified the new task to which he was called by God—to become "the father of a multitude of nations" (Genesis 17:4).

Abraham lived with his father's family in Mesopotamia (now called Iraq). He was led by God to leave his homeland

28

to go into a new country, whose location he did not know but which God promised to show him.

This faithful response to God on Abraham's part was in the form of a covenant, a binding agreement. The covenant is a very important part of the Old Testament religion. In Genesis 9 we read of the first covenant of which there is mention in the Old Testament—the promise God made to Noah that the human race would not be destroyed, the sign of which was to be the rainbow in the sky. This covenant with Abraham was to be remembered in circumcision, which became a necessary rite to be undergone by all Hebrew males from this time on.

> And I will establish my covenant between me and you and your descendants after you throughout their generations for an everlasting covenant, to be God to you and to your descendants after you. And I will give to you, and to your descendants after you, the land of your sojournings, all the land of Canaan, for an everlasting possession; and I will be their God (Genesis 17:7–8).

When they had arrived in Canaan, Abraham and Lot, with their respective herdsmen and families, found it necessary to live separately. Lot chose the Jordan Valley region. You can read the story of what happened to the cities of Sodom and Gomorrah, located in the region Lot chose, in Genesis 18 and 19. Abraham and his clan took up their residence in Canaan, the Promised Land.

Isaac

Abraham and Sarah, his wife, were now very old. It grieved them that they had no son to whom to pass on their inheritance and to receive God's promises to Abraham and his descendants. In a time of despair over having no heir, Abraham had a child, Ishmael, by Sarah's serving-maid, Hagar, with

Sarah's full consent and encouragement. This child, however, was not permitted by God to become Abraham's heir because he was the result of Abraham's temporary loss of faith in God's promises. Later, Sarah, although beyond the normal age of child-bearing, conceived a child to whom they gave the name Isaac (Genesis 16 and 17).

The proof of Abraham's faith is given in the famous story in Genesis 22 of how he took his only heir to an altar where he was about to sacrifice him alive when God intervened to stay his hand. Human sacrifice was practiced in those ancient times. The fact that Isaac was not sacrificed indicates the conviction on the part of the writer that God never intended to allow Abraham to make such a sacrifice, but Abraham's willingness to go to the extreme to show God how much he trusted Him is the center of that story.

Isaac's marriage to Rebekah is one of the "arranged romances" of the Old Testament, about which we can read in Genesis 24. She was brought from Abraham's ancestral homeland in Haran (Mesopotamia) so that Isaac might marry someone from his own tribe. It was not considered good for Isaac to marry a Canaanite woman, for that would have broken the line of descent within the covenant family. This is an example of the ancient custom whereby decisions about marriage partners were made not by the young people themselves but by their parents.

Jacob

Isaac and Rebekah had two sons, the twins Esau and Jacob. Since Esau was the first-born, he normally would have been Isaac's heir, but Jacob deceived his father and received Isaac's blessing (Genesis 27). It used to be thought that when words of a blessing or a curse were said, the words themselves produce the intended result; hence when Isaac blessed Jacob instead of Esau, even though he did not realize he was doing so, what he did held firm. Esau later became the "founder" of the nation of Edom, whereas Jacob continued the line from Abraham and became the ancestor of Israel.

Jacob's deception did not go unpunished, however, and he fled for his life. In Genesis 28:10–22 we read of a spiritual experience that came to him. In some remote place he lay down to sleep, taking a stone for a pillow. While he slept, he dreamed that a ladder reached from earth to heaven; on it the angels of the Lord ascended and descended. The Lord stood at the top of the ladder and spoke to Jacob:

> I am the Lord, the God of Abraham your father and the God of Isaac; the land on which you lie I will give to you and to your descendants; and your descendants shall be like the dust of the earth, and you shall spread abroad to the west and to the east and to the north and to the south; and by you and your descendants shall all the families of the earth bless themselves (Genesis 28:13–14).

When Jacob awoke, he said, "Surely the Lord is in this place. . . . This is none other than the house of God, and this is the gate of heaven" (verses 16–17). He set up a memorial pillar, using the stone on which he had slept, and called the place Bethel (the house of God). He also vowed that he would dedicate a tenth of all his possessions in the future to the Lord— an early evidence of the custom of "tithing" still prevailing among many Church people.

Finally Jacob arrived in Mesopotamia (Abraham's ancestral homeland), where he married Leah and Rachel. Speaking of romance, read in Genesis 29 how Jacob really wanted to marry Rachel, whom he loved at first sight, as it were, but found that Laban, their father, had deceived him by insisting that he first marry the older daughter, Leah. What did he do? He worked another long seven years in order to win Rachel, the "beautiful and lovely." We must remember that in these early times husbands took a number of wives. The ideal of one man and one woman in marriage was not fully achieved until Christianity, centuries later, insisted that this was God's intent for us.

The children of Jacob included the twelve sons who became the ancestors of the Twelve Tribes of Israel. Before his death, Jacob was renamed Israel, by whom the whole people would henceforth be named. We read, happily, in Genesis 32–33 that the brothers Jacob and Esau managed to bury the hatchet and make a new compact of friendship between them.

5

ISRAEL IN EGYPT

CHAPTERS 37 THROUGH 50 of Genesis tell the story of Joseph, the son of Jacob, who became a central figure in the next phase of Israel's history.

Probably you remember vividly the story of how Joseph was punished by his brothers because he had the unfortunate habit of thinking too highly of himself. In his dreams he would see himself as being more important than the rest, so that they would bow down to him. Is this a tendency for younger children of almost any family, to want to try to create a secure place for themselves in comparison with their older brothers and sisters? In any event, Joseph was seized and bound one day when he came to see his brothers in the fields at Dothan. At first several of them were inclined to kill Joseph, but Judah urged them instead to sell Joseph to a group of Ishmaelites who came by. These traders carried him away to Egypt where he was bought by Potiphar, an officer of Pharaoh, the Egyptian king.

Joseph's destiny was to be a glorious one. Evidently he was recognized as a capable young man and for that reason fared better by far than most slaves. Among other things, he got the reputation of being able to interpret dreams. This led to his being brought into the presence of the Pharaoh himself, who was being troubled by perplexing dreams. Joseph interpreted one of Pharaoh's dreams as meaning that a famine would shortly come to the land, causing a great shortage of food. Pharaoh was so much impressed with the young man's prediction that he appointed Joseph second in command of the kingdom. He was assigned the job of setting up a store of food to serve the people during the predicted famine.

The famine came. There was food in Egypt, enough for all. Even people from neighboring countries came there seeking relief. Among those who came were Joseph's brothers who went down from Palestine. They recognized Joseph only when he identified himself to them, although he of course knew who they were. During a long interview he learned a great deal about the present state of his father's household. Then came a reconciliation after the long separation. Note how the words put on Joseph's lips refer once again to God's providential direction of Israel. It is God who has used the bad situation of the selling of Joseph into slavery to bring forth His purpose:

> As for you, you meant evil against me; but God meant it for good, to bring it about that many people should be kept alive, as they are today (Genesis 50:20).

After Four Hundred Years

We have seen how Joseph, carried to bondage in Egypt, became a saviour of Egypt. Once in the promise to Abraham, God had said that Israel would be a source of blessing to the nations. Here, in what we have seen happened to Joseph, the purpose of God could be observed as it worked itself out through the succession of leadership from Abraham down. Of course, while the events were taking place, people did not always realize that God's purpose was at work; but in looking back at events, they could see how God had been fashioning things by His providence.

It was thus through Joseph that the Hebrews had been brought into Egypt. After Joseph identified himself to his brothers, he talked to them and earnestly urged them to bring their father Jacob down to Egypt. The Pharaoh was pleased with the idea also and offered to give the father and brothers of Joseph special lands in Goshen where they could continue their occupation of herding.

Those who came into Egypt were a comparatively small number of people. We read in Genesis 46:8–27 a list of members of the tribe who came along with the patriarch Jacob (Israel). They were fruitful and multiplied, we are told (Genesis 47:27). In fact, they multiplied to a very great extent indeed in the next four hundred years.

In Exodus 12:40 we read: "The time that the people of Israel dwelt in Egypt was four hundred and thirty years." We know nothing about the years between the death of Joseph and the appearance on the scene of Moses, save that "the descendants of Israel were fruitful and increased greatly; they multiplied and grew exceedingly strong; so that the land was filled with them" (Exodus 1:7).

Finally the memory of Joseph was lost in official circles of Egypt. Doubtless he had been remembered for a long time as a great leader in the country, and as long as that remembrance lasted, his fellow-Hebrews would have had a measure of prestige and security. They had been good citizens, had prospered and made a place for themselves. All that, though, was now a thing of the past for "there arose a new king over Egypt, who did not know Joseph" (Exodus 1:8). With that line their changed situation is ominously introduced.

The new king "who did not know Joseph" evidently was especially displeased over the fact that the Hebrews had grown into such a sizable element in the population. Apparently also he resented that they were able to wield a large measure of influence. At any rate, he decided to start a program of oppression. He made them slaves. Forced by taskmasters to do the king's bidding, the Hebrews, once the favored relatives of the prime minister (Joseph), now carried heavy burdens, toiling in the construction of the new cities of Pithom and Raamses which the Pharaoh was building.

Even in the face of slave labor, the Hebrews continued to thrive as far as numbers were concerned. Next the Pharaoh decided to try to get rid of newborn males and issued orders that all boy babies among the Hebrews should be cast into the Nile River. The Hebrews' condition got worse and worse.

At what time of history are we now speaking? The scholars are not all agreed, but many think that the Exodus—which was the solution to the problem of bondage in Egypt—took place in the reign of a Pharaoh named Rameses II, who was on the throne from 1290 to 1224 B.C., roughly three thousand two hundred years ago.

6

TOWARD THE PROMISED LAND

MORE THAN FOUR HUNDRED years after Joseph's death a new leader emerged. This was Moses. At the time the Hebrews were enslaved in Egypt, this young man was growing up in the Egyptian court circles. He had been taken under the protection of one of the princesses, who found him lying in the basket where his mother had put him in the reeds by the river bank. His mother had hidden the baby for three months to save him from death under the Pharaoh's decree about killing Hebrew male babies, but she took the chance that someone would find him and care for him. Her hopes were rewarded.

When the child Moses grew up, he remembered that he was a Hebrew and felt sympathetic toward his own people. When he saw a taskmaster beating one of the Hebrew slaves, he impulsively killed the Egyptian. Then he knew that in order to live he would have to flee from Egypt. He went into the land of Midian.

While on the desert of Sinai, Moses married the daughter of Jethro, a Midianite. It is thought that some of Moses' later religious ideas may have been partially influenced by practices of the Midianites.

Meditating one day on the mountainside of Sinai (also called Mt. Horeb), Moses had an unusual experience. He saw a wayside bush bursting into flame and heard God speak to him from the burning bush:

> I have seen the affliction of my people who are in Egypt, and have heard their cry because of their taskmasters; I

37

know their sufferings, and I have come down to deliver them out of the hand of the Egyptians, and to bring them up out of that land to a good and broad land, a land flowing with milk and honey, to the place of the Canaanites, the Hittites, the Amorites, the Perizzites, the Hivites, and the Jebusites. . . . Come, I will send you to Pharaoh that you may bring forth my people, the sons of Israel, out of Egypt (Exodus 3:7–10).

After hesitating at first, feeling very unequal to the task to which he felt God was calling him, Moses heeded the divine command. Going back to Egypt he decided to confront Pharaoh with the demand that the Hebrews should be permitted to leave Egypt. You may recall the vivid spiritual, "Go Down, Moses . . . Let My People Go," which expresses Moses' demand to the king. One after another he performed signs and wonders on behalf of God. Then came the event called the Passover. As the story is told, the first-born child in each Egyptian family was stricken dead one night, but the Hebrew homes were spared that tragedy. Finally, the Pharaoh gave in, permitting Moses (even being eager by this time to do so, perhaps) to take the Hebrews away from his country. Ever since, the Passover has been regarded as a most important Hebrew religious festival, celebrated annually, as we celebrate Easter, for example.

"When your children say to you, 'What do you mean by this service?' you shall say, 'It is the sacrifice of the Lord's passover, for he passed over the houses of the people of Israel in Egypt, when he slew the Egyptians but spared our houses,' " And the people bowed their heads and worshiped (Exodus 12:26–27).

After Moses and the Hebrews left, however, the Pharaoh changed his mind. He decided to send troops after them to try to stop their escape.

We should pause a moment to say something about the

route Moses took after the Hebrews left Egypt. There were two courses open to them. One would have been the coastal road, used by caravan traders and soldiers. It was fortified in places by the Egyptians, hence it would have been a foolhardy route for Moses to take. They had open one other course— crossing the wilderness toward what the Scriptures call the Red Sea. This, however, is not the Red Sea we know on our maps. Rather, the wilderness route took them toward a marshy lake named Timsah, which is really a narrow stretch of water, very shallow, near the end of the Gulf of Suez. The words in the Exodus account really should be translated "Reed Sea" or "Sea of Reeds." Most scholars agree that the crossing of the so-called Red Sea took place in that region.

We cannot be sure how many people were involved in the Exodus from Egypt. Exodus 12:37 refers to "six hundred thousand men on foot, besides women and children." In addition there were other people, "a mixed multitude," who had attached themselves to the Hebrews, not to mention considerable cattle. It looks as if the estimate of numbers given here is far too big. There would not have been enough resources in the country to which they were moving to take care of them if there had been that many.

In the Wilderness

The terrain over which the Hebrews had to pass was not easy to cross. Apart from the physical exhaustion of the journey on foot, the travelers faced added problems: lack of water in the parched desert places, scarcity of things to eat, the danger of wild beasts.

It wasn't long before there were mumblings of dissatisfaction among some of the people. They complained that Moses had brought them out on a fool's trip. Would it not have been better had they stayed in Egypt where things, though bad, were not nearly so miserable as in this wilderness?

> Would that we had died by the hand of the Lord in the
> land of Egypt, when we sat by the fleshpots and ate bread
> to the full; for you have brought us out into this wilderness
> to kill this whole assembly with hunger (Exodus 16:3).

Yet the people were sustained by the provision of manna
which they found on the ground each morning and by water
which flowed from a rock struck by Moses' rod. These pro-
visions are recorded in the biblical account as proof of God's
intervention to assure the people an arrival in the Promised
Land.

Another problem they had to contend with was the constant possibility of attacks from unfriendly dwellers in the
region they were trying to enter. They were regarded as
invaders, naturally, by the Amalekites and others who in-
habited the land. We read in Exodus 17:8–16 about one
rather big battle with the Amalekites. It is interesting to read
because it shows evidence of a primitive idea about the place
of the leader in the battle. Joshua is the army captain and
leads the actual fighting, but standing on the hilltop, over-
looking the proceedings, is Moses. Whenever Moses holds up
his hand, the Hebrews have the better part of the struggle;
when his hand falls down, Amalek prevails. Finally Moses
grows tired from holding his hand up so long. Whereupon
his brother, Aaron, and Hur assist him in holding up the
hand until sunset, by which time Joshua has the battle under
control.

At a later time, after the Ark, which was thought to contain God's presence, had been built, the Ark itself was
carried into battle. The success of Israel's military campaigns
was thought to depend on the presence of the Ark in the
midst of the warriors; its absence could produce defeat. It has
been pointed out that already, in this early stage of their
community life, Israel was developing a concept of "holy
war." It was felt that in order to achieve His purposes, God

would uphold the people in warfare. If victory came to them, it would be only because Yahweh, their God, had made it possible.

God Their Leader

Throughout this period of moving toward the Promised Land, the leaders (if not always the people) were sure that God was leading them. Even as He had made it possible for them to cross the Reed Sea to escape from the Egyptians in their chariots, so He would make it possible for them to enter that Land of Promise, the same territory that had been given to Abraham and his heirs. They must have been held up by the high hopes of the future as well as by the sense of relief at having escaped from slavery. The whole record of the Exodus and the wilderness wandering is written in terms of a divine-human drama. Not only are the people moving toward the Promised Land, it is God Himself who moves with them as the active director of their journey.

And the Lord went before them by day in a pillar of cloud to lead them along the way, and by night in a pillar of fire to give them light, that they might travel by day and by night; the pillar of cloud by day and the pillar of fire by night did not depart from before the people (Exodus 13: 21-22).

Eventually the wilderness wanderers came to an oasis near Mt. Sinai, the one on whose very banks Moses had had his burning bush experience. Here they set up a camp. Now, as we shall see, they began to look back on their experiences as a people and to think through the meaning of it all. Why had they been delivered from Egypt? Why, in spite of miseries and unhappiness, had they been sustained? What was the meaning of their common life? Here, too, they were to get a new understanding of covenant and law.

7

COVENANT AND LAW

Now we come to one of the most important matters in the whole Pentateuch—the covenant at Sinai. It looks as if Moses deliberately led the people toward Mt. Sinai, for we find a reference as early as Exodus 3:12. God speaks to Moses: "But I will be with you; and this shall be the sign for you, that I have sent you: when you have brought forth the people out of Egypt, you shall serve God upon this mountain." Remember, this conversation between God and Moses took place at the time of the burning bush incident, on the very slopes of Mt. Sinai itself, to which he would return with the people when they were freed from Egypt.

The material which we shall be considering in this chapter is found in Exodus, from Chapter 9 to the end of the book; in Leviticus; and in Numbers 1–10.

Immediately upon arriving at Sinai and making camp, Moses is said to have gone to the mountain, where he entered into dialogue with God. This must be construed, certainly, as meaning that Moses was praying to God, for prayer is basically conversation, with or without words, between man and God. In this encounter with God, Moses heard words that were both a recollection of the fact that they had been brought up from Egypt and an indication as to what was going to happen next in the making of the covenant between Israel and the Lord:

"Thus you shall say to the house of Jacob, and tell the people of Israel: You have seen what I did to the Egyptians, and

42

how I bore you on eagles' wings and brought you to myself. Now therefore, if you will obey my voice and keep my covenant, you shall be my own possession among all peoples; for all the earth is mine, and you shall be to me a kingdom of priests and a holy nation. These are the words which you shall speak to the children of Israel" (Exodus 19:3–6).

The response of the people was their willingness to say "yes" to God. It was as if they were saying "Amen" or "So be it" when they answered Moses' report of what God expected of them: "All that the Lord has spoken we will do" (Exodus 19:8).

There is an important element in the covenant between God and Israel: the "If." God promises to remain faithful to Israel, to exalt them so that they shall be "a kingdom of priests and a holy nation," but this will depend on their faithfulness in keeping the conditions of the covenant.

The Law

In the account that follows we have the story of the giving of the Law to Moses. Some of you may have seen the Cecil B. DeMille movie, *The Ten Commandments.* There the Exodus 19 account is shown in awesome literalness with lots of fire and smoke. Actually, this is the kind of situation that no one could possibly portray in art or movie. The true awesomeness of it is the awareness on the part of the biblical writer that he is describing the most solemn moment in Israel's history since the Exodus—the meeting of God with man in terms of the Law by which man is shown how to live in company with God. Only the God-appointed leader, Moses, was able to meet with God on the holy mountain. He it was who had to be the medium through which the Law was transmitted to men.

The actual ceremony in which the covenant was accepted

by the people is described in Exodus 24. Here we see how blood sacrifice of animals was closely linked to the covenant idea, and we know how animal sacrifice played a big part in the Temple worship at Jerusalem in the years ahead.

The covenant takes the form of the various laws set forth in Exodus 20:23—23:32 in addition to the Ten Commandments. Usually these laws are referred to as the Covenant Code. There are further laws in later chapters of Exodus and in Leviticus and Numbers that have mostly to do with priestly practices. It is thought by scholars that these later laws belong to a period after Moses, though they were included in the Exodus material by the editors.

When we use the Ten Commandments in church (the Prayer Book requires that they be said during Holy Communion at least monthly), or whenever we say them to ourselves, we can have the thrilling awareness that we are voicing words that come down to us from the time of Moses. Our Lord summarized the Law and the Prophets in the words we use in every celebration of the Holy Communion:

> Hear what our Lord Jesus Christ saith. Thou shalt love the Lord thy God with all thy heart, and with all thy soul, and with all thy mind. This is the first and great commandment. And the second is like unto it; Thou shalt love thy neighbour as thyself. On these two commandments hang all the Law and the Prophets (The Book of Common Prayer, p. 69).

The Ten Commandments are also listed in another place in the Bible—Deuteronomy 5. We shall have occasion to explain what the book of Deuteronomy is when we take up "The Great Reform" in Chapter 16. Although the book of Deuteronomy is placed as one of the books of the Pentateuch (the Five Scrolls), it belongs to a much later time, as we shall see. Meanwhile, you might want to compare the two versions of the Ten Commandments by looking up Deuteronomy 5:6–21. Note also the summary of the Commandments as given in the famous Shema, Deuteronomy 6:4–5, which is still repeated daily by a devout Jew. The word *Shema* is the Hebrew for the first word of the Hebrew text. Can you see here the indebtedness of our Lord to the Shema, which He must have known from earliest childhood? Compare the Shema with the Summary of the Law as we use it in the Holy Communion.

Other Ancient Codes

We know that not only Israel, but other ancient peoples as well had codes of law. One of the most famous of these is the Code of Hammurabi, who was king of the First Babylonian Dynasty, 1728–1686 B.C. This code is inscribed on a stone called a *stele* which is on display in the famous Louvre Museum in Paris. The difference between the covenant law of Israel and the other influential laws of surrounding nations was this: the covenant involved the whole of Israel's life. It applied to rich and poor alike, considered equal in God's sight. Before God all life was thought of as sacred. So the Law of Israel was not like the laws a ruler might lay down, or a legislature, for the governing of a people. Both the laws referring to individual behavior and the conduct of the state have to do with life under the government of God.

The remainder of the book of Exodus refers to the laws set forth for the construction of the Tabernacle where the worship of the people would be celebrated. These are quite detailed descriptions as to what all the furnishings should be like.

Leviticus contains the priestly laws regarding ritual and ceremony. It has much to say about what is clean and unclean, what the priesthood must do and not do, what is holy for the individual and for the people of Israel. In Chapter 16 there is a description of the ceremonies of the Day of Atonement, a high and solemn day which is still observed among the Jews.

8

INTO THE PROMISED LAND

WHEN WE OPEN the book of Numbers, we find a continuation of the laws which we have grown used to seeing in the latter part of Exodus and in Leviticus.

When we come to Numbers 10:11, however, we return to the account of the Israelites' movement toward the Promised Land. The time spent in camp near Mt. Sinai was, as we have said before, a time of establishing laws, thinking through the covenant, and—in a true sense—catching their breath after the difficult Exodus from Egypt.

The Israelites had now embarked on a struggle to get control of the land into which they hoped to move as permanent settlers. The story from here on is a narrative of conquest, alternate victories and defeats, and finally a fairly sure settle-ment in the land they had longed for. Actually, however, the life of Israel was never settled, as far as absolute security and permanence is concerned, but isn't that true of almost every nation one can think of? The journey from here on sounds more like a constant movement of armed troops than was the earlier journey from Egypt to Sinai. The Ark was carried in formal procession ahead of the people. Whenever the Ark set out, Moses would say: "Arise, O Lord, and let thy enemies be scattered; and let them that hate thee flee before thee." And when it rested, he said, "Return, O Lord, to the ten thousand thousands of Israel" (Numbers 10:35–36).

There are recorded in Numbers the restlessness and scan-dals that arose among the people because of the problem of getting enough food to eat and Miriam's and Aaron's dislike of Moses because he had married a native (Cushite) woman, although actually they were perhaps jealous of his exclusive leadership.

The story of the sending of spies into the land of Canaan to find out what it looked like and what chances there were of their getting in is given in Numbers 13. The task that they had to face looked hard indeed. Some were in a hurry to get the conquest over with quickly, but these hasty ones were badly defeated, as Moses had warned them would be the case (Numbers 14:39–45). Korah, Dathan, and Abiram were others who turned their back on Moses' leadership.

The writer of Numbers suggests that because the people rebelled against Moses, they would have to wander in the wilderness for forty years. During this time they made their headquarters at an oasis called Kadesh-barnea (south of Canaan). It was during these years that Israel was welded more and more into a unified people, in spite of the fact that the people lived under strained, unpromising circumstances that led often to misunderstanding. Scholars have pointed out that on the surface it would seem as if the people should have failed to keep together at all, what with tribal rivalry, jealousy, insecurity, and all the rest of the things that characterized their life in the wilderness; but the fact is that the covenant bond held strongly, and the people were learning through their experience what God intended for those whom He had chosen for His own purposes.

Conquest

The fortresses guarding Canaan on the south were too big for the Israelites to conquer, so they had to find another way to get into the land on which they had set their eyes. They decided to try to go up through Transjordan to enter Canaan from the east. This was no mean task, for already there were settled peoples of Semitic stock, related to the Hebrews but having their own national life—Edom (remember Esau!), Moab, Sihon (the kingdom of the Amorites), and Ammon.

Each of these nations posed a military problem to Israel. Their first big victory was over the Amorites. Then they took on Og, the king of Bashan.

Numbers inserts (Chapters 22–24) an interesting story about Balaam. That man was a Syrian whom the King of Moab had asked to curse the Israelites. (Remember that it was thought the words of a blessing or a curse were effective in and of themselves when spoken.) Instead of cursing Israel, Balaam was led to recognize the superiority of Yahweh, the Hebrew God.

> How can I curse whom God has not cursed?
>> How can I denounce whom the Lord has not de-
>> nounced? . . .
> Who can count the dust of Jacob,
>> or number the fourth part of Israel? (Numbers 23:8, 10).

Incidentally, you can also read in this story about the talking ass, which is seemingly more famous than Balaam himself in popular remembrance!

Why is the book of Numbers called that? In it are recorded details of two census-takings (the first is described in Chapters 1–4, the second in Chapters 28–36). These chapters do not make very exciting reading, but they do give a picture of the distribution of the population according to the Twelve Tribes.

In Numbers 27:12–22 we can read the sad word to Moses that he will not be permitted to enter the Promised Land himself. In his place he is to see Joshua called as his successor to lead the people into Canaan and commissioned in a ceremony before Eleazar the priest. Note that it is the Lord who is said to have appointed Joshua, rather than there having been an election by the people.

In Chapters 1–12 of the book named after Joshua we read of the final conquest of Canaan. Under Joshua's leadership (Moses now having died), the Israelites attacked and conquered Jericho, then Ai, and finally the interior. Once having achieved the military conquest, they proceeded to divide the land according to the tribes.

The Gathering at Shechem

Joshua 24 is an extremely important chapter for here we read of Joshua's gathering of the leaders of all the tribes at Shechem. He reminds them of the long history of Israel, from Abraham through the Exodus and up to the recent conquest of Canaan. He ends on this great note—a kind of renewal of the covenant:

> Now therefore fear the Lord, and serve him in sincerity and in faithfulness; put away the gods which your fathers served beyond the River, and in Egypt, and serve the Lord (Joshua 24:14).

The people with one voice insist that they will serve the Lord. Here they were, in the Promised Land, renewing the covenant, this time on a grand scale as a formal tribal confederacy. From now on they were to face many temptations to forsake the god of Israel and serve the exciting gods of the Canaanitish people among whom they were to live. Israel's history was to be a constant affirming of God and a turning away from Him to serve other gods. At the heart of their religion was always the remembrance of the covenant, made with Abraham, with Moses, and now renewed under Joshua.

PART II
THE PROPHETS

9

WHEN THE JUDGES RULED

As we have mentioned earlier, the first five books of the Old Testament were regarded by the Jews as the basic sacred literature. Thus they were called, taken as a whole, the Torah, a Hebrew word that means *Law* or *Teaching*. We also have referred in Part I to the book of Joshua. Technically, Joshua was included in the Hebrew Bible under the heading "Former Prophets," along with Judges, I and II Samuel, and I and II Kings. Since the material in the book of Joshua, however, continues the narrative in the first five books, the first six taken together are often viewed as a unit of material. The name given to the first five books is *Pentateuch,* as we have seen, meaning *Five Scrolls.* If we include Joshua, the six books collectively are called the *Hexateuch* (meaning *Six Scrolls*).

Before we go on to consider the book of Judges, let us stop for a minute to look at a few verses in Deuteronomy 26 which summarize for us the way in which the Hebrews would remember their greatest experience of God's guidance when they shared in a religious ceremony. It was the custom to present the first fruits of the harvest before the priest at the place of worship. The worshipper would say to the priest, "I declare this day to the Lord your God that I have come into the land which the Lord swore to our fathers to give us." Then the priest would take the basket of produce and put it down before the altar. (See Deuteronomy 26:1–4.) The worshipper would say these words:

A wandering Aramean was my father; and he went down into Egypt and sojourned there, few in number; and there he became a nation, great, mighty, and populous. And the Egyptians treated us harshly, and afflicted us, and laid upon us hard bondage. Then we cried to the Lord the God of our fathers, and the Lord heard our voice, and saw our affliction, our toil, and our oppression; and the Lord brought us out of Egypt with a mighty hand and an outstretched arm, with great terror, with signs and wonders; and he brought us into this place, and gave us this land, a land flowing with milk and honey. And behold, now I bring the first of the fruit of the ground, which thou, O Lord, hast given me (Deuteronomy 26:5–10).

We can see in this short passage how the chief point of remembrance is the Exodus from Egypt. The "wandering Aramean" refers to the patriarch Jacob. That is the only reference to the earliest days of the Hebrews. The big event was the deliverance from Egypt and the promise God fulfilled to bring them into the Promised Land. At the time of the annual harvest festival, they especially remembered how God had chosen them, guided them, and brought them there.

Continuing Struggles

Although the people of Israel were able to establish themselves in Canaan, they still had many struggles ahead. The twelfth and eleventh centuries B.C. were a time when Israel had to make efforts to get supreme control of the land and to find a way to deal with the practices of the Canaanite peoples among whom they were now living. This is the period referred to in Ruth 1:1 which gives us our chapter heading, "in the days when the judges ruled." The book of Judges is the history of this difficult period.

Although Joshua had led the people into the forming of a kind of tribal confederacy, as we have seen, this did not provide a firm government. We read in Judges 17:6 "In those days there was no king in Israel; every man did what was right in his own eyes." This same line is repeated as the very last verse in the book (Judges 21:25). This refers to the ups and downs of these long years. The people alternately remembered the covenant with God and forgot it. As the story is told in this book, we see how, one after another, leaders were raised up to deliver the people from the enemies who had oppressed them because they had been unfaithful to the covenant.

We have to understand something about the situation in Canaan. The natives of that region worshipped a kind of nature deity called the Baal. There were also female deities called the Ashtaroth. It was thought by them that if the local Baal, the real owner of the land, could be pleased by the people, the lands would be fertile and produce good crops. The people of Israel were surrounded by these worshippers of the Baal. They were constantly being tempted to follow the practices of their neighbors. Archeologists have dug up little statues of these regional gods, especially of the Ashtaroth. Eventually, the Israelites kept these in their homes. We know that children were even named after the gods. For example, Gideon had another name, Jerub-baal, which actually means *Let Baal contend.* (See Judges 7:1.)

As the story is told in Judges, the struggle was between a strict obedience to the God of Israel and the temptation to serve the gods of the region. The Hebrew God demanded absolute obedience, as had been established in the first of the Ten Commandments: "You shall have no other gods before me" (Exodus 20:3).

The Judges

Now who were the Judges? The term is rather difficult for us, because we use the word "judge" in a different sense from which the Bible uses it. We think of a judge as a person appointed or elected to preside over disputes taken to the law courts. Among the Israelites, the "judge" was first of all a military leader. He was able to have authority to decide important questions because he had first proved himself a strong leader in one of the tribes. He or she (for one famous judge, Deborah, was a woman) served almost as a kind of king, thought to have divine authority. Thus Gideon, one of the judges, is said to have had "the Spirit of the Lord" come upon him (Judges 6:34).

When we read Judges, we are likely to get the impression that one followed the other in a line of succession. Actually, it did not happen in quite that way. What we really have is a series of incidents or events each of which is centered around some important leader, and these are woven together into a continued story.

You will enjoy reading these old stories. Life was rough in those ancient times, and the Bible does not hesitate to describe conditions as they were in all their barbarism and cruelty. You will read about Ehud, who killed Eglon, king of Moab, "a very fat man," as the king rested alone in his roof chamber (Judges 3:12–30). Judges 4 and 5 tell the story of Deborah and Barak and their defeat of Sisera and the Canaanites at Megiddo. This is given in poetry in the fifth chapter, in prose in the fourth. Note that the details differ although the incident is the same.

Midianite camel-riders would attack the settlements of the Israelites so that the people were always in danger of losing what they had gained. Judges 6 through 8 tells the heroic exploits of Gideon in ridding Israel of that menace. The Ammonites were routed by Jephthah, who vowed that if he won the battle, he would sacrifice the first person to meet him upon his return home. We read in Judges 11 the sad story of the sacrifice of his only child, a young daughter, in the keeping of his vow. Another group of invaders were the Philistines, who were able to come by sea to the Mediterranean shores. The judge who arose to combat them was Samson, the man of great physical strength, whose tragic story is told in Chapters 13 through 16.

10

"GIVE US A KING"

SAMSON WAS NOT a military leader. The Philistines were far from being dislodged from power; in fact, they became stronger year after year. In the face of their might, the Israelites were unable to hold their own even when the Ark was carried into battle.

Shiloh had become the central place of worship for the Israelite Confederacy of Tribes. Once a year a pilgrimage was made to that place, where Eli, the High Priest, was in charge. When the Philistines were seeming to win a battle, as a last resort the sons of Eli took the Ark into the fray. Although the Israelites raised their voices with a great shout so as to frighten the Philistines, the invaders discovered they were superior in arms and even captured the Ark, which they carried away to their own territories.

Archeologists have found out an interesting fact in this connection. The incident we mentioned above is the last in which Shiloh is referred to. The reason is that Shiloh was destroyed in that battle of Ebenezer during which the Ark was captured. The central place of worship of the confederacy was burned to the ground. A long time later, when people were saying that the Temple at Jerusalem would last against all enemies, the prophet Jeremiah made a reference back to Shiloh:

> Go now to my place that was in Shiloh, where I [the Lord] made my name dwell at first, and see what I did to it for the wickedness of my people Israel (Jeremiah 7:12).

The narrative tells that the news of the capture of the Ark was so shocking to Eli that the ninety-eight-year-old High Priest "fell over backward from his seat by the side of the gate; and his neck was broken and he died" (I Samuel 4:18).

Samuel

Times of tragedy and defeat sometimes result in the turn of the tide. The people of Israel had been encouraged time and time again by leaders who would arise to guide and direct them in the way that would restore them to wholeness. Looking back on these leaders, the biblical writers were sure that it was God who had sent them for times of crisis in order that His purposes might be fulfilled.

Such a one was Samuel. The story of the boy Samuel, the son of Elkanah and Hannah, and how he was put into the service of Eli the High Priest at an early age, ministering to the Lord, is probably familiar to you from your Church School studies of past years. You can read about him in I Samuel 1, 2, and 3. We read:

> And Samuel grew, and the Lord was with him and let none of his words fall to the ground. And all Israel from Dan to Beersheba knew that Samuel was established as a prophet of the Lord (I Samuel 3:19–20).

During the time that Samuel was growing up in Eli's service, the Philistines were getting established in Canaan as Israel's chief invaders.

Who was Samuel, really? In one sense he was a prophet, like others called "prophet" about whom we shall hear more later—those who announced the will of God to the people of Israel—but he also can be called the last of the judges. He seems to have been trying to find a way to meet the changing political situation. As we have seen, there were many judges, none of whom was succeeded by his own children. Samuel saw, however, that some kind of continuity was needed in order to have a more stable government. Israel would go to pieces unless some leadership could be assured from generation to generation. So he appointed his own sons as judges.

The leaders of the people were not pleased about this. They wanted leadership that would continue, but they did not regard Samuel's sons as equal to the task. Thus they came to Samuel and insisted that what they really wanted and needed was a king.

Samuel did not like this idea at all. The writer puts on the lips of the Lord Himself an objection to this suggestion about having a king, for a king would mean that they were rejecting the Lord as king over them. Samuel was very strong in his warnings to the people:

> These will be the ways of the king who will reign over you: he will take your sons and appoint them to his chariots and to be his horsemen, and to run before his chariots; and he will appoint for himself commanders of thousands and commanders of fifties, and some to plow his ground and to reap his harvest, and to make his implements of war and the equipment of his chariots. He will take your daughters to be perfumers and cooks and bakers. He will take the best of your fields and vineyards and olive orchards and give them to his servants. . . . And in that day you will cry out because of your king, whom you have chosen for yourselves; but the Lord will not answer you in that day (I Samuel 8:11–18).

Finally the people persuaded the judge Samuel that it was right that they should have a king. The record suggests that even the Lord heeded the people's persuading, saying to Samuel: "Hearken to their voice, and make them a king" (I Samuel 8:22).

This desire for a king was no new thing. Earlier they had wanted to make Gideon king, but he had refused the office. The reason kingship was resisted so long lay exactly here:

God alone was king, and not even a nation in its greatness and power could take the place of the reign of God. Even after the monarchy was established, prophets would arise to warn the kings when they were not acting in accordance with the rule of God.

Saul Becomes King

The first king of Israel was Saul, whose reign is described in I Samuel 13–31. Note that he was anointed king by Samuel, who met him on that day when he was out in the fields looking for some lost animals belonging to his father, Kish. It was Samuel who called the leaders of the people together and announced to them the choice for king. So modest was the young man that they found him hiding among the baggage (I Samuel 10:22). Not everyone thought highly of the new king, for some said, "How can this man save us?" (I Samuel 10:27). Soon after, however, he led valiantly in battle against the Ammonites and proved himself a strong military leader.

Samuel was disappointed in Saul, whom he thought undependable. Probably no one would have pleased Samuel in the position of king, for Samuel did not believe the people should have a king anyway. Because Saul had disobeyed what Samuel regarded as God's commands (see I Samuel 15:17–23), Samuel declared that he could no longer be king, and that another would be chosen in his place. That one was going to be David, who was first brought into the palace to play the lyre to soothe Saul at a time when he was feeling greatly upset. Saul liked David so much that he took him into his service as his personal armor-bearer. The story of David's friendship with Jonathan, Saul's son, is beautifully told in Chapters 18ff. The jealousy Saul felt toward David becomes more and more intense as the story unfolds, until finally, in Chapter 31, we read of Saul's death by his own hand in a battle with the Philistines.

11

THE GLORIOUS KINGDOM

THE BOOK OF II Samuel takes up at the death of Saul and
Saul's sons. Already David's future is sealed. He will become
king of the Southern part of Israel. Before we go into the
details of his career from this time on, we should read that
tremendous piece of literature in Chapter 1 which is David's
lament over Saul and Jonathan:

> Thy glory, O Israel, is slain upon thy high places!
> How are the mighty fallen! . . .
>
> Saul and Jonathan, beloved and lovely!
>   In life and in death they were not divided;
> they were swifter than eagles,
>   they were stronger than lions. (II Samuel 1:19, 23).

David began a new era in the history of Israel. Although
Saul had been king in fact, actually he operated very much
within the tradition of the older tribal confederacy. Under
David there began steps which led to the development of a
strong central government.

David was a clever leader and has been called a master
politician. During Saul's latter years he had been exiled in
the wilderness, but soon after Saul's death we find that he
placed himself in just the right position to be acclaimed king.
The northern tribes continued to be loyal to Saul's son,
Ishbaal, a weak person who did only what the general,
Abner, wanted him to do. Abner had a quarrel with Ishbaal
and decided to turn Saul's former northern holdings over to

David, along with Michal, Saul's daughter, who was to become David's wife. This marriage into Saul's family established David's claim even more strongly to the remainder of Saul's kingdom.

Next David sought to strengthen the independence of his kingdom. At first he had been a kind of vassal king, taking orders from the Philistines, but soon he embarked on a military drive to get rid of the Philistines in Canaan.

Another stroke of genius was his capture of Jerusalem, where the Jebusites long had held a fortress thought to be too strong for any invader to capture. This city, once captured, was to become his capital.

> And David dwelt in the stronghold, and called it the city
> of David. And David built the city round about . . . And
> David became greater and greater. . . . (II Samuel 5:9–10).

In the typical fashion of attributing developments to God's purpose, the development of Jerusalem and David's increasing power are attributed to "the Lord, the God of hosts [who] was with him" (II Samuel 5:10). Jerusalem was an important part of David's scheme. It had been neutral as far as the tribes were concerned, since it had been held by enemies, and for that reason became a symbol of the growing national unity of Israel.

Jerusalem was destined to be not only a political capital (like Washington, D.C., in our country), but also a religious center for the people's spiritual hopes and destinies. David had the Ark installed in Jerusalem, and eventually the magnificent Temple of Solomon was to be built as a central location for the people's worship of God. This, too, tended to unify the people very much, for one of David's problems originally was to cement the people into one national solidarity. For the Hebrews, from time immemorial, the covenant with God was the one thing that made them distinct from all other peoples.

A Highly-Organized Kingdom

David's kingdom grew ever more brilliant. Wealth resulted from increasing trade with surrounding nations. The city of Jerusalem became a handsome place with capital and royal buildings designed by Phoenician architects. The very measures David and his counsellors took to strengthen the monarchy were also the cause of unhappiness and misery for many. In the old tribal confederacy there had always been a strong measure of independence on the part of the various tribes. A national census was taken by David. Information thus gathered was used for setting up new taxes and assigning men to serve in the army. There was even set up a system of forced labor which the people resented greatly.

Revolution was in the air. A son of David's named Absalom was the center of one revolt in the south, and in the north a man named Sheba started a similar movement:

> We have no portion in David, and we have no inheritance in the son of Jesse; every man to his tents, O Israel! (II Samuel 20:1).

Although David held his own in these crises, they showed that not all was well with the kingdom.

An interesting piece of material is inserted into II Samuel 9 through 20. These chapters come from what appears to be a court history. Similar material is contained in I Kings 1 and 2. Here we see in straightforward writing some of David's weaknesses. Although he was a man of great strength of character in some situations, in other situations he was selfish and cruel. This is seen in the way he contrived to get rid of Uriah the Hittite, a faithful subject, in order to be able to marry Bathsheba, Uriah's wife.

Nathan, the prophet, was furious when he learned about the treachery of David toward Uriah. In II Samuel 12, we read how Nathan came to the king and told a little story about a rich man who took a poor man's lamb to prepare a meal for a traveler instead of using his own flock. Hearing the story, David bursts out, "As the Lord lives, the man who has done this deserves to die; and he shall restore the lamb fourfold, because he did this thing, and because he had no pity." Then Nathan, having caused the king to condemn himself already, pointed to David, saying: "You are the man!" (II Samuel 12:1–15).

David died a rather pathetic old man. Within his family there had been conflict, coming to its height in the rebellion of Absalom against his father. The kingdom that was so glorious in many ways was destined to last only a little time more because by the end of the reign of David's son, Solomon, the son of Bathsheba, it was split into two.

Yet such is the power of tradition that David's weaknesses, even though recorded frankly in Scripture, were eventually overlooked. Succeeding generations looked back to David as the greatest of leaders. It was remembered chiefly that he had been one who "administered justice and equity to all his people" (II Samuel 8:15). It was recalled that he had established the great city where God's worship was centralized for the people Israel. Finally, in times of desperation after the fall of Jerusalem itself, it was thought that from the line of David there would spring a Messiah, an anointed one. (*See* Isaiah 9:6–7.)

12

A KINGDOM DIVIDED

ISRAEL ALWAYS had been a people gathered together on the basis of a covenant with God. With the rise of the monarchy under Saul and especially under David, a new element had entered the history of the people. They were now not only a religious people; they had become a politically unified people. The objections Samuel had raised against having a king were in a sense being realized, for the people had discovered that the king would indeed make strong demands on them. Their freedom would not be primarily a freedom in relationship to God but one that the king could grant or refuse.

Nevertheless, Israel was destined to have a continuing period of prosperity under King Solomon, who succeeded David. It was a time of glory, too, of a kind, so that Solomon's reign was always remembered in those terms.

It wasn't a foregone conclusion at David's death who would become the next king. I Kings 1 and 2 tell the story of the struggle between the half-brothers, Adonijah and Solomon, for the throne. Incidentally, those two chapters are the end of the court history which began, you recall, in II Samuel. The material telling about Solomon's reign evidently comes from another source. I Kings 3 through 11 gives information taken, according to I Kings 11:41, from "the book of the acts of Solomon," which contained, probably, much more material than was preserved in I Kings.

We have enough information to give us some interesting facts about Solomon. Later generations were sure that Solomon's prosperity must have been due to his having been a wise person. They wrote that Solomon was interested at the outset of his reign in being as wise as possible. He prayed to God, "Give thy servant therefore an understanding mind to govern thy people, that I may discern between good and evil; for who is able to govern this thy great people?" (I Kings 3:9). The reply from the Lord assured Solomon that he was to have not only a wise and discerning mind, but also "what you have not asked, both riches and honor, so that no other king shall compare with you, all your days." Yet there is a condition attached to this promise! Solomon was to have these blessings only if he would walk in the Lord's ways, keeping His commandments and statutes (I Kings 3:12–14).

Solomon's reputation for wisdom is shown in the little incident preserved in Chapter 3:16–28. Two mothers each had a child. One of the children died, and both mothers claimed the living child. Solomon showed his wisdom by ordering that the child be cut in half. The child's real mother cried out that the living child should be given to the other woman. Thus it was revealed who the child's real mother was.

A Magnificent City

Solomon's father David had been busy consolidating the empire and getting rid of as many remaining enemies as possible. Solomon, on the other hand, was interested in building up the prosperity of his kingdom and making its civilization as magnificent as possible. The building of the royal palace and the Temple were part of an over-all plan to make Israel as splendid a kingdom as anything else in the ancient world.

Chapters 5:1 through 9:9 give details of the construction of the Temple. It was finally dedicated with great pomp and ceremony as sacrifice was offered before the Lord. The words of Solomon to the people reach a lofty religious level, as he reminds them of God's goodness to them since the time of the promises to Moses:

> Let these words of mine, wherewith I have made supplication before the Lord, be near to the Lord our God day and night, and may he maintain the cause of his servant, and the cause of his people Israel, as each day requires; that all the peoples of the earth may know that the Lord is God; there is no other. Let your heart therefore be wholly true to the Lord our God, walking in his statutes and keeping his commandments, as at this day (I Kings 8:59–61).

Solomon was not above tricky dealings. He made a shrewd bargain to give certain cities to Hiram, king of Tyre, in exchange for building materials, but Hiram was not pleased with them. He used forced labor in the twenty years of building. Furthermore, he "loved many foreign women . . . from the nations concerning which the Lord had said to the people of Israel, You shall not enter into marriage with them (I Kings 11:1–2). These marriages brought entanglements with the worship of these pagan wives' religions.

For these sins Solomon was warned that his kingdom would be torn from him. Yet this would not be in his own day, for the sake of his father David; yet certainly it would happen in his son's day (I Kings 11:9–13).

Division of the Kingdom

For all his later reputation as a man of wisdom, Solomon in his lifetime was actually a tyrant, a very selfish and cruel ruler. The end result was revolution.

The story of the division of the kingdom starts with I Kings 12. After Solomon died, his son Rehoboam made a trip to Shechem, in the north, to be recognized as king by the northern tribes. (He was already installed as king in the southern part of the kingdom.) The northern tribes insisted that the load his father Solomon had put upon them be made lighter.

The young king replied clearly that he had no intention to make things easier for the people: "My father made your yoke heavy, but I will add to your yoke; my father chastised you with whips, but I will chastise you with scorpions" (I Kings 12:14). This refers to Solomon's use of forced labor to which we made a reference above. The son would be harsher than the father!

Immediately the tribes of Israel in the northern part of the kingdom withdrew. Here was the beginning of the end of the united kingdom.

> What portion have we in David?
> We have no inheritance in the son of Jesse.
> To your tents, O Israel!
> Look now to your own house, David (I Kings 12:16).

About 922 B.C. a man named Jeroboam, who had been involved in the revolutionary movement, was made king of Israel (the northern kingdom's ten tribes). The other two tribes, in the southern part of the kingdom, Judah and Benjamin, were to be known from this time on as Judah. The glorious kingdom of David in so short a time had become a divided kingdom—and in the future were to lie more strife and confusion.

13

WHAT HAPPENED IN ISRAEL

WHEN WE READ the accounts in Kings and Chronicles, we must remember that we are reading what might be called "edited history." We do not always have a straightforward account of events exactly as they happened, but we do have the interpretation of the events as they looked to the historian from where he stood. "Objective" history in the sense of setting down exactly what happened is practically impossible to write. Just think of how a particular football game might look to you, as a loyal supporter of your own school team, and how it would look to a loyal supporter of the other school's team. You would both have certain "facts" to report, such as the place and hour of the game, the names of the players and referees, the score at different points of the game, and—of course—the final score! That final score would mean victory to one of you and defeat to the other. You couldn't help writing it up from the standpoint of the way you or your school were involved in it.

Thus in the accounts of the kings who reigned in Israel and Judah, we have the writer's own slant. He lists them by name, and in the order of their reigns, but he also adds here and there certain comments on how they looked to him. The fact is, there were so many kings that it is very difficult to keep them all straight. In fact, we do not need to do so, for it is only the more important ones whose names we shall want to remember. As an aside, it *is* interesting to note some of the comments of the writer. For example, there is Nadab, who reigned over Israel for two years. Of him it is said: "He did what was evil in the sight of the Lord, and walked in the way of his father, and in his sin which he made Israel to sin" (I Kings 15:26). Of Omri it is said that he "did more evil than all who were before him" (I Kings 16:25). The writer wanted to make it clear that any king who failed to keep the covenant was evil indeed.

King Ahab

The mention of Omri brings us to a very important king of Israel. His son, Ahab, came to the throne around 876 B.C. and reigned for almost twenty years. Omri had made war against the Moabites for many years, having defeated them and added them to his empire. He also had done his best to prevent the spread of the powerful Syrian armies. One way he sought to strengthen his position was to make friends with Phoenicia. It was to the daughter of the king of Phoenicia, a princess named Jezebel, that Ahab was married.

We remember Ahab largely because it was during his reign that the prophets Elijah and Micaiah arose, and these are important figures.

The Elijah stories are found in I Kings 17–19 and 21. Elijah appeared on the scene at the time Jezebel was having a great deal of influence on the religion of Israel. She had been used to the worship of the Baal of Tyre, a city in Phoenicia. Now since Ahab wanted to please his wife and also please her Phoenician royal family, he built a temple to Baal, fully equipped with an idol and all that was required for Baal-worship. This caused Elijah's anger to rise to fever point since it was so great a sin in the sight of the Lord.

The background seems to have been something like this. Jezebel had brought a number of prophets of the Baal from her home country, and these were receiving their living from the national treasury of Israel. This is what is meant by

Elijah's reference to "the four hundred and fifty prophets of Baal and the four hundred prophets of Asherah [the Baal mother goddess], who eat at Jezebel's table" (I Kings 18:19). Apparently Jezebel wanted to do all she could to make the Baal-worship popular in her new country.

There is a dramatic meeting between the king and Elijah. When the king sees the prophet, he calls out, "Is it you, you troubler of Israel?" Elijah protests: "I have not troubled Israel; but you have, and your father's house, because you have forsaken the commandments of the Lord and followed the Baals" (I Kings 18:17–18).

The Contest

Elijah asks that these prophets be assembled at Mount Carmel so that he might have a contest with them to show who is the greater, Yahweh or the Baal. To the gathered people of Israel Elijah said:

> How long will you go limping with two different opinions? If the Lord is God, follow him; but if Baal, then follow him (I Kings 18:21).

There had been a long drought. The prophets of Baal had been insisting that only through their rites could the god who controls fertility and rain be reached, and many of the Israelites evidently had given in to that belief. Elijah was interested in proving once and for all that Baal-worship was nonsense, that God alone controlled all the powers of the world.

The description of the contest in I Kings 18:20ff. is some of the most exciting reading in the Old Testament. Elijah challenges the Baal prophets to prove whether their god could cause fire to consume an animal prepared for sacrifice. They indulge in their elaborate ceremonies all morning, but nothing happens. There is a trace of humor in the way Elijah chides them about their god: "Cry aloud, for he is a god; either he is musing, or he has gone aside, or he is on a journey, or perhaps he is asleep and must be awakened" (I Kings 18:27). Their continued efforts, however, produce no results.

Then Elijah calls the people to draw near him. He takes stones (twelve in number, symbolizing the Twelve Tribes of Israel) and repairs the altar of the Lord that had been thrown down. He takes water and pours it on the wood. Why would he have done that if he wanted the wood to burn? Many scholars feel that this symbolizes the result hoped for by the appeal—the end of the drought. Then he appeals to God: "Answer me, O Lord, answer me, that this people may know that thou, O Lord, art God, and that thou hast turned their hearts back" (I Kings 18:37). The fire comes. The people are amazed and convinced, crying out, "The Lord, he is God; the Lord, he is God" (I Kings 18:39). The prophets of Baal are seized and killed. Then comes the desired result: the rain pours from the skies.

All of this, naturally, makes Jezebel the more furious, and she threatens to have Elijah killed. Elijah flees into the wilderness. On Mt. Horeb (Sinai), the very place where Moses received the revelation of God's Law, Elijah has the experience of encounter with God described in I Kings 19:9–18. He is told that he should appoint Elisha as the prophet to carry on his work.

The next time Elijah meets King Ahab is in connection with Naboth's vineyard. Ahab has wanted a piece of property owned by Naboth, who does not want to relinquish it. Jezebel urges Ahab to get it any way he can. The result is that Naboth is accused wrongly of having committed treason and cursed God, and is stoned to death. The prophet confronts the king with his sin and pronounces the doom of Ahab and his house in the strong language of I Kings 21:20–24.

Micaiah

The other important prophet whom we see in relation to Ahab is Micaiah. Do not confuse him with Micah, the prophet whose name is used in one of the books of the Old Testament. We read about Micaiah in I Kings 22.

King Ahab and the king of Judah, Jehoshaphat, met to discuss the possibility of going to war jointly against Syria in order to capture a place called Ramoth-gilead. The southern king asked that before they proceed the prophets be consulted, as was the custom before any big decision was made. Ahab, who wanted the war, summoned four hundred prophets who enthusiastically predicted that the Syrians would be routed in the war. Jehoshaphat was not yet convinced and asked if there were not yet another prophet who should be consulted. Micaiah's name was mentioned. When he was brought in, he refused to take Ahab's view of the matter, insisting that if Ahab entered this war, he would be destroyed, the four hundred other prophets notwithstanding.

The importance of Micaiah is that he insisted that he would have to speak the word of God as it had come to him, even though this meant opposing the king, the nation, or the people. The other prophets were in a sense employed to say what the king wanted them to say, but Micaiah, like Elijah and like Amos and Hosea and the others whom we shall be considering, insisted on putting God's truth first.

14

A WARNING TO REPENT

THE DEATH OF AHAB brought to an end the dynasty of Omri.
Then followed, in the Northern Kingdom of Israel, a series
of kings beginning with Jehu, who had been an army general
in the battles with Syria over Ramoth-gilead. Jehu was
anointed king by Elisha, who had taken Elijah's place as a
chief prophet. (See II Kings 9:1–13.)

Thus we come to another king, Jeroboam II. Not a great
deal is said about him in II Kings 14:23–29, but we know
from findings of archeologists that his reign was a time of
great prosperity. It was the last period of "greatness" for the
Northern Kingdom. The excavations at the capital city,
Samaria, show that a high standard of wealth prevailed,
doubtless concentrated in the hands of the ruling classes.
Trade with Phoenicia was at its height, and Jeroboam II controlled the trade routes to Syria and Arabia. The Baal-worship
that had reached enormous popularity under Ahab was still
common, and many of the people apparently felt that the
worship of the sacred bulls, sacrifices at the Baal altars, and
similar religious practices were the cause of the prosperity.

If it was a prosperous time, however, the prosperity was
limited to the few as against the many. The common people
were suffering from burdens of taxation and low wages.

It was during Jeroboam II's reign that two very important
prophets made their appearance: Amos and Hosea.

Who Were the Prophets?

We should pause a moment to say something about who the prophets were. Earlier we mentioned that there were a group of ecstatic soothsayers who surrounded practically every royal court in the ancient world. These were the men to whom kings would turn to try to get light on what moves should be made in battles and other matters pertaining to their kingdoms. With Elijah, Micaiah, and Elisha we saw another kind of prophet who was more concerned with making pronouncements according to God's will as it had been revealed to him. These were the "troublers of Israel," men who were willing to run the risk of saying unpopular things if that was what God inspired them to say.

The prophets were not fortunetellers, or predicters of future events, in the way we sometimes use the word "prophet" today. They were deeply involved in the present and stated how things would work out in the near future if certain patterns of action were followed. They were "spokesmen for God" who proclaimed the will of God for His people Israel in the actual happenings of history through which their people were passing.

Amos

The book bearing the name of Amos gives us more of Amos' concerns than it tells us about the man himself. We know only a few details about him. The first verse of the book states that he "was among the shepherds of Tekoa." He was active during the reign of Jeroboam II, near the end of that king's life, say around 750 B.C. He is one of the group whom we refer to as the great eighth-century prophets.

From Amos 7:1–15 we learn a little more about the prophet. He apparently was a native of Judah, for Tekoa was a village south of Jerusalem. The priest of Bethel, Amaziah, told Amos that he ought to get himself out of Israel. If he wanted to prophesy, he ought to go south and do it there without troubling Israel. Amos had been saying hard things about Jeroboam's future: "Jeroboam shall die by the sword, and Israel must go into exile away from his land (Amos 7:11).

Amos replied to Amaziah, mincing no words:

> I am no prophet, nor a prophet's son; but I am a herdsman, and a dresser of sycamore trees, and the Lord took me from following the flock, and the Lord said to me, 'Go, prophesy to my people Israel.' Now therefore hear the word of the Lord (Amos 7:14–16).

He denied any interest in being a "professional prophet," one of those who have a kind of "official" standing. In other words, he wanted it to be known that he was speaking the truth as he saw it purely because God had commissioned him to do so. He wasn't prophesying because that was the way to earn a living.

Amos' words were written down either by himself or by a circle of friends who especially cherished them. The other prophets before him, Elijah and Elisha, were remembered only through the oral tradition, but here we have the actual words of the prophet. We must not assume that the book was written all in one piece. It seems to contain various pronouncements (called *oracles*) which he gave at different times, and these were finally put together into a scroll that became the present book of Amos. He spoke his words at Bethel, a religious center, and maybe at Samaria. Although he was thinking first of all of the Northern Kingdom, he felt justified in doing so because he had in mind the entire "people of Israel . . . the whole family which I [the Lord] brought up out of the land of Egypt" (Amos 3:1).

Amos was speaking to a people whose leaders felt that their present prosperity under Jeroboam II was a guarantee of God's continuing favor. Meanwhile, however, Assyria's power was a growing threat to Israel, even though it was not cause for immediate alarm. The people were not irreligious; in fact, they were *very* religious, for religion had been tied in with the national political life in such a way that people felt God must surely be blessing their present practices. Were they not His chosen people?

What Amos tried to do was to remind the people that being God's chosen ones meant that they had a great responsibility before God. They could not merely be content with outward trappings of religion; they needed an inner renewal of spiritual life. There was a great deal of talk about the coming Day of the Lord—the time when God would reign in His full splendor, but they misunderstood what the Day of the Lord would really involve:

> Woe to you who desire the day of the Lord!
>   Why would you have the day of the Lord?
> It is darkness, and not light;
>   as if a man fled from a lion,
>   and a bear met him;
> or went into the house and leaned with his hand against the
>   wall,
>   and a serpent bit him.
> Is not the day of the Lord darkness, and not light,
>   and gloom with no brightness in it? (Amos 5:18–20).

When the day of the Lord comes, men will be judged as to whether they have kept the covenant inwardly, in their hearts. Amos went on to say, in the words of God:

> I hate, I despise your feasts,
>   and I take no delight in your solemn assemblies.
> Even though you offer me your burnt offerings and cereal
>   offerings,
>   I will not accept them,
> and the peace offerings of your fatted beasts
>   I will not look upon.

Take away from me the noise of your songs;
   to the melody of your harps I will not listen.
But let justice roll down like waters,
   and righteousness like an everflowing stream (Amos
   5:21–24).

Hosea

Hosea prophesied during the last year of Jeroboam II's life, 746 B.C., and for some years afterwards, in the years just before Israel's final collapse in 721 B.C.

Hosea was married to a woman named Gomer, by whom he had three children with strange, symbolical names, two of which were "Not-pitied" and "Not-my-people." Gomer was unfaithful to him, leaving him for other lovers. Legally he could have divorced her, but instead, for love of her, he received her back as his wife. From this personal experience he learned a lesson about God's ways with the people Israel.

Just as Hosea had married Gomer in love and had cared for her, so God had chosen Israel and in the covenant with them had offered them His love and care. They, like Gomer, had turned unfaithful. They had forsaken Him to go after other gods. The result will be that "the children of Israel shall dwell many days without king or prince, without sacrifice or pillar. . . ." (Hosea 3:4). Like Gomer, they will be reduced to utter destitution. Yet God, being love, will receive them back when the children of Israel seek Him again, even as Gomer was received back into Hosea's life and household. "And they shall come in fear to the Lord and to his goodness in the latter days" (Hosea 3:5). Israel's flaw had been that the people failed to acknowledge God in all their life; they had become like a wife separated by her wrong choices from the husband who had loved her.

Assyria's legions will overrun Israel and destroy the nation. The people will be punished for their sins. Yet even in this punishment, God will not forsake them, but through it, will bring them back ultimately to Himself. After the punishment, they will see that God has permitted this to happen to them only because they could not learn in any other way how He really loved them. In the end:

> I will heal their faithlessness;
>   I will love them freely,
>   for my anger has turned from them. . . .
> They shall return and dwell beneath my shadow,
>   they shall flourish as a garden;
>   they shall blossom as the vine. . . . (Hosea 14:4, 7).

15

COUNSELOR TO KINGS

WHILE JEROBOAM II was king of Israel, the Southern Kingdom, Judah, was being ruled by a descendant of King David,
Uzziah. The Northern Kingdom had been by far the leading
part of the divided people of Israel, more prosperous, more
in the center of things in the ancient Near East. In one respect, however, Judah had an advantage. Instead of having
a succession of various ruling houses, as happened in Israel,
the crown of David had kept the smaller nation in control
with far fewer ups and downs. We can read about Uzziah's
reign in II Kings 15:1–7 and in II Chronicles 26. He was
apparently a very successful king. He had pioneered in developing copper and iron mining, agriculture, trade with Arabia,
and a more modern type of army.

Israel started to decline rapidly after Jeroboam II died
and was conquered by the Assyrians, as we mentioned, in
721 B.C. At this same time the Kingdom of Judah was about
as secure as she had ever been since the days of David and
Solomon, except for one thing: Assyria's rising power. Under
an emperor named Tiglath-pileser, Assyria started a cam-
paign the aim of which was to get control of the whole Fertile
Crescent area.

We first hear about Isaiah in the year in which King Uzziah
died, 742 B.C. He continued to be an important prophet for
over forty years, through the reigns of Ahaz and Hezekiah.
During Isaiah's time, he saw many important events take
place, all of which were centered around Assyria's rise to

power. The chief thing Isaiah had to combat was the forming of alliances with Israel, Egypt, and Syria in an effort to keep back Assyria. He thought that just as Israel's efforts to do this brought nothing but ruin, so Judah also would finally succumb to the Assyrian power.

The Book of Isaiah

In reading the book called Isaiah there are several things we must keep in mind. First, not the whole book is by Isaiah himself. The first thirty-nine chapters represent his own work. When his pronouncements were not being listened to at one point in his career, he retired from public view for a while to write down his ideas so that, when the time was ripe, they would be ready to be made public. These writings were kept by some of his disciples (pupils and followers) and eventually put together in a scroll. It is probably true that Chapters 34 and 35 were not by Isaiah either, for these are more like Chapters 40–66, which were written about two hundred years later during the Exile, as we shall see, by an unknown writer usually referred to as the Second Isaiah. When the scrolls of Isaiah were put together by his disciples, at a much later time, this material from the later Isaiah was put together with Isaiah's.

The Man Isaiah

Although we know little about Isaiah, it seems that he was a city man, possibly having been brought up in Jerusalem. He seems to have had a great many friends in the royal court, so it is usually thought that he may have come from a well-known or prominent family. His feelings were bound up with the throne of David and his descendants.

Chapter 6 gives us the story of his call to be a prophet. It is beautifully written and is one of the favorite passages in the book of Isaiah. The young man is worshipping in the

Temple. There he beholds a vision of the Lord in all His glorious majesty. The heavenly beings call to one another saying:

> Holy, holy, holy is the Lord of hosts; the whole earth is full of his glory (Isaiah 6:3).

These are the very words echoed in the Holy Communion when the priest says or sings:

> Therefore with Angels and Archangels, and with all the company of heaven, we laud and magnify thy glorious Name; evermore praising thee, and saying,

followed immediately by the *Sanctus,* priest and people together repeating:

> HOLY, HOLY, HOLY, Lord God of hosts, Heaven and earth are full of thy glory: Glory be to thee, O Lord Most High. Amen (The Book of Common Prayer, p. 77).

Isaiah's reaction to this vision is a feeling of personal unworthiness and sin. He cries out, "Woe is me! For I am lost; for I am a man of unclean lips, and I dwell in the midst of a people of unclean lips; for my eyes have seen the King, the Lord of hosts!" (Isaiah 6:5); but his soul is forgiven by the symbol of the burning coal from the altar that one of the seraphim uses to touch his mouth, and when he hears the voice of the Lord asking "Whom shall I send, and who will go for us?" he immediately replies, "Here I am! Send me." Then Isaiah receives his commission. It is not an easy one. He is to give the word of God to people who will hear but not understand (Isaiah 6:6–13).

Isaiah was to preach constantly on the theme that the Lord judges His people. In the Song of the Vineyard he compared Israel and Judah to a garden in which the Lord had made a "pleasant planting," but instead of justice, bloodshed grew

up, instead of righteousness a bitter cry. (See Isaiah 5.) Like
Amos, Isaiah proclaimed the coming Day of the Lord:

> And the haughtiness of man shall be humbled,
>   and the pride of men shall be brought low;
>   and the Lord alone will be exalted in that day.
> And the idols shall utterly pass away (Isaiah 2:17–18).

When King Ahaz was tempted to make alliances with
foreign powers in order to protect his threatened throne,
Isaiah warned him not to put his trust in kings but in God.
"Take heed, be quiet, do not fear, and do not let your heart
be faint," he said to Ahaz (Isaiah 7:4). He was sure that over
and beyond the affairs of men the supreme purposes of God
would be carried out, even though it might mean, as he told
King Hezekiah, that "all that is in your house . . . shall be
carried to Babylon; nothing shall be left, says the Lord"
(Isaiah 39:6).

The Child

Isaiah has always played an important part in Christian
thinking because of his prophecy concerning the birth of a
child who would be God's pledge that He is with His people.
(See Isaiah 7:14.) This child would be born of the line of
David.

> For to us a child is born,
>   to us a son is given;
> and the government will be upon his shoulder,
>   and his name will be called
> "Wonderful Counselor, Mighty God,
>   Everlasting Father, Prince of Peace."
> Of the increase of his government and of peace
>   there will be no end,
> upon the throne of David, and over his kingdom,
>   to establish it, and to uphold it

with justice and with righteousness
   from this time forth and for evermore.
The zeal of the Lord of hosts will do this (Isaiah 9:6–7).

This was the beginning of the Jewish thought concerning a Messiah who would be sent by God to be the Redeemer of His people. The early Christians, many centuries later, were convinced that in Jesus Christ this prophecy was fulfilled and God had actually come to earth to redeem them, bringing all mankind a deliverer from sin and death.

Because of passages like that quoted above, Isaiah has been used a great deal in Christian devotion. It is interesting that the portion of Scripture appointed to be read for the Epistle on the feast of the Annunciation of the blessed Virgin Mary, March 25 each year, is Isaiah 7:10–15. (See the Book of Common Prayer, p. 235.)

The Prophet Micah

While Isaiah centered his prophecy in the Jerusalem area, another man, less influential but great in his own way, was raising his voice about conditions in the country districts. This was Micah. He lived at the same time as Hosea and Amos. In many ways his message was like Amos'. He was distressed over the persecution of the poor by the wealthy landowners who "covet fields, and seize them; and houses, and take them away; they oppress a man and his house, a man and his inheritance" (Micah 2:2). He wanted justice to reign and said that those "who hate the good and love the evil, who tear the skin from off my people, and their flesh from off their bones" will finally "cry to the Lord, but he will not answer them . . . because they have made their deeds evil" (Micah 3:2–4).

Micah's own work is in the first three chapters. The remaining chapters were written by someone whose name we do not know (like the Second Isaiah). Here is included the very famous line:

> He has showed you, O man, what is good;
>   and what does the Lord require of you
> but to do justice, and to love kindness,
>   and to walk humbly with your God? (Micah 6:8).

16

THE GREAT REFORM

ISAIAH IS SAID in the Jewish traditions (though not in the
Bible itself) to have been martyred during the reign of King
Manasseh, who succeeded Hezekiah. It was during Manasseh's
reign that the prophets were forbidden to speak or act at all.

Hezekiah had heeded Isaiah by avoiding an alliance with
Assyria, but Manasseh did just the opposite. He even turned
his back against the religious loyalties of the people of Israel,
thus starting a period of pagan religion under royal approval.
II Kings 21 gives details about his program. Manasseh died
in 642 B.C. After two years of his son Amon's reign, a boy-
king named Josiah, only eight years old, came to the throne.
In the year 621 B.C. that boy, then grown into early man-
hood, was destined to start a religious reform of the greatest
importance.

Zephaniah

Before we discuss the Great Reform of Josiah, we should
take a brief look at the prophet Zephaniah. He became the
first prophet to make an important appearance after the long
period of seventy-five years or so since the prophets had been
forced by Manasseh to keep quiet. It is thought that he, like
Isaiah, was a resident of Jerusalem.

What was on his heart and mind? Like Amos and Isaiah
years before, Zephaniah proclaimed that the Day of the Lord
was about to come. This would be a time of judgment and
terror:

> The great day of the Lord is near,
>   near and hastening fast;
> the sound of the day of the Lord is bitter . . .
> A day of wrath is that day,
>   a day of distress and anguish,
> a day of ruin and devastation,
>   a day of darkness and gloom . . . (Zephaniah 1:14–15).

He complains that the people of the city are blind to the Lord's coming; her officials are "roaring lions"; her prophets are "wanton, faithless men"; her priests "profane what is sacred, they do violence to the law" (Zephaniah 3:3–4). The Lord is righteous and just, however, and He will restore the people after they have been judged, through "those who are left in Israel," for not all would be destroyed. (See Zephaniah 3:13.)

What is the reason for Zephaniah's concern? He could not have been referring to Assyria, for now Assyria was no longer on top of the international scene. Maybe he was referring to an expected invasion of barbarian armies from the north (the Scythians). In any event, he urged those who still had time to repent and look to their ways in the sight of God.

It is interesting to note that a great hymn of the Christian Church during the Middle Ages was based on Zephaniah's Day of the Lord. (You will want to look up Hymn No. 468 in *The Hymnal*.)

Josiah's Reform

King Josiah, freed from worry about Assyria, decided on a policy of getting rid of many things that reminded the people of their former great enemy. We can read about his efforts in II Kings 22–23 and II Chronicles 34.

Among other things, repairs were started at the Temple. A scroll that had been lost track of for a long time was found and delivered to the king's secretary by Hilkiah, the High Priest. The secretary brought it to Josiah. When the king had studied the book and verified it by consulting Huldah, a prophetess, it was realized all around that this was indeed the Book of the Law. Josiah was horrified to recognize that the Law of God (the Torah) had been neglected all these years. At a solemn assembly he read the book of the covenant to the people.

> And the king stood by the pillar and made a covenant before the Lord, to walk after the Lord and to keep his command- ments and his testimonies and his statutes, with all his heart and all his soul, to perform the words of this covenant that were written in this book; and all the people joined in the covenant (II Kings 23:3).

The king was as good as his word to God. A reform was begun which aimed at getting rid of all foreign types of worship. Idols were destroyed, "high places" (altars at various places outside Jerusalem) were abolished, and the worship of the nation was completely centralized at the Temple in Jeru- salem.

Do we know what was the book found in the Temple during the repairs? The scholars believe that it refers to the part of the Law contained in Chapters 12 to 26 of the book of Deuteronomy. Because of this, Josiah's reform movement has sometimes been called the Deuteronomic Reformation.

Why was the book lost? No one knows the answer to this. It is possible that it was not really a lost book at all but a revi- sion of ancient laws that had been made privately during the long reign of Manasseh in the hope that at some future time someone in authority would find it and do something about bringing the people back to the Mosaic religion.

The Book of Nahum

One of the smaller and least-known books of the Old Testa- ment comes from the period of Josiah's reign when Assyria had lost its dominant power. Nineveh, the capital of Assyria, had fallen in 612 B.C. The writer rejoiced over the fact that Nineveh had been ruined:

> The river gates are opened,
>   the palace is in dismay. . . .
> Nineveh is like a pool
>   whose waters run away . . . (Nahum 2:6, 8).

> Your shepherds are asleep,
>   O King of Assyria;
> All who hear the news of you
>   clap their hands over you (Nahum 3:18–19).

This small writing shows the form religious nationalism was able to take in expressing its pride and hope.

17

THE FALL OF A KINGDOM

JOSIAH HAD DREAMED of bringing about a new united kingdom of the people of Israel, but he did not reckon with the facts of the case. Although Assyria had been defeated, Egypt still had ambitions to get back her former glory as a great empire. Josiah decided to gamble by challenging the Egyptians in a battle at Megiddo. As it happened, he lost the gamble and also his life. The Egyptians won that battle, and Judah became a vassal of Egypt. Soon the Egyptians went on farther to take on Babylonia, the rising empire. That was the end of *their* hopes. At the famous battle of Carchemish in 605 B.C. the Babylonians under Nebuchadnezzar II sent the Egyptians into full retreat. Babylonia was now the complete master of the ancient world, and it was not to be many years before Judah fell under her enormous power. In 597 B.C. Jerusalem, under King Jehoiakim, fell to Nebuchadnezzar. Finally, in 586 B.C. under King Zedekiah who started a rebellion against Babylonia, Jerusalem was completely destroyed by the Babylonian king, even the walls and the Temple being torn down to the foundations. The Exile, about which we shall hear later, had begun.

Jeremiah

One of the really great prophets lived his life against this historical background. Actually, he began his prophesying during the early years of King Josiah's reign. He lived a long time, to the very end of the kingdom of Judah. The book called by Jeremiah's name contains material from both the earlier and later parts of his career.

Note in Jeremiah 1:6 how he, like Moses and Isaiah, feels unequal to the call to do God's work: "Behold, I do not know how to speak, for I am only a youth," but the Lord assures him that the words he needs will come to him. He is called to a high and holy task:

> See, I have set you this day over nations and over kingdoms,
> to pluck up and to break down,
> to destroy and to overthrow,
> to build and to plant (Jeremiah 1:10).

His earliest prophecy is contained in chapters 2:1 through 4:4. Readers who are familar with Hosea often notice how much like Hosea's words this material seems to be. Jeremiah refers to the early years of Israel, when God had received the people's love as a husband his bride. Across the years Israel has forgotten the covenant. God pleads with Israel to return, to have healing of their faithlessness. (See Jeremiah 3:22, 4:1–2.) He was pleading for a reform, an inward spiritual reform first of all, not merely the kind of reforms that Josiah was going to put into effect.

The Burned Scroll

Jeremiah had a secretary named Baruch. About the year 605 B.C. when Jehoiakim (Josiah's son) was ruler, Jeremiah decided to dictate to Baruch his various oracles. Jeremiah was alarmed about Babylonia's growing power and was sure that there would be an attack from the north. From his memory of more than twenty years' prophesying, Jeremiah spoke these words for his secretary to write down.

Then Baruch took the scroll to the Temple where he read it. The leaders were stunned to hear the words of Jeremiah that God would punish the people of Judah by sending Babylonian invaders into their country. They took the scroll to the king. There is a wonderful picture of Jehoiakim sitting before the fireplace in his winter palace. To show his contempt for the prophet, as the scroll was read to him, he would cut off column after column, throwing it into the fire. You can read this in Chapter 36 of the book of Jeremiah. Meanwhile Jeremiah and Baruch had fled for their lives, and in a secret hiding-place Jeremiah started all over again to dictate his oracles to Baruch. This is why the book has been preserved for us even though Jehoiakim burned the original in his winter palace.

Jehoiakim aroused Jeremiah's anger. Already Josiah's Deuteronomic Reform (see the preceding chapter) was dying down, and the present king was permitting all kinds of heathen religious practices to flourish once more, even letting idols be set up in the Temple.

Jeremiah preached the coming doom of Judah. There would be no hope in political alliances with Egyptians or with Babylonians.

> For even if you should defeat the whole army of Chaldeans [Babylonians] who are fighting against you, and there remained of them only wounded men, every man in his tent, they would rise up and burn this city with fire (Jeremiah 37:10).

False prophets were prophesying lies in the name of the Lord; people were no longer trusting one another; idols were being worshipped throughout the country. No, there was no hope, save that the people should receive God's punishment. Only then could they be healed.

> Your ways and your doings
>   have brought this upon you.
> This is your doom, and it is bitter;
>   It has reached your very heart (Jeremiah 4:18).

Jeremiah did not only talk. He also used "signs." You can read about one of these signs, the linen waistcloth, in Jeremiah 13:1–11; another, the clay flask, is found in Chapter 19.

Jeremiah never gave in on his conviction that it was utterly foolish to stand out against the Babylonians. During the siege of Jerusalem, Zedekiah, who was now the king, sent a message asking Jeremiah's opinion. Even then, at that last-ditch stand, he was sure that God was acting through the Babylonians to punish the people:

> Behold, I set before you the way of life and the way of death. He who stays in this city shall die by the sword, by famine, and by pestilence; but he who goes out and surrenders to the Chaldeans [Babylonians] who are besieging you shall live and shall have his life as a prize of war. For I have set my face against this city for evil and not for good, says the Lord: it shall be given into the hand of the king of Babylon, and he shall burn it with fire (Jeremiah 21:8–10).

Zedekiah was torn between following Jeremiah's advice or holding out as his advisers insisted. Chapters 37 and 38 tell of the secret conferences held between the king and the prophet. The king did not change his mind. His pathetic end is told in chapter 39:1–8. Jeremiah was let out of prison, after the siege was over, on orders from Nebuchadnezzar.

The book of Lamentations is a series of dirges over the fall of Jerusalem. It is connected with Jeremiah only because it deals with the same fall of the city that he experienced—hence his name is attached to it.

Habakkuk

A little book of only three chapters gives the prophecy of Habakkuk. This seems to have been written about the time of the battle of Carchemish in 605 B.C. Habakkuk is upset by the growing power of the Babylonians and is led to ask the question, Why? If the Lord is the controller of life, why can these invaders win so much through their military might? He goes up to a watchtower, and there in his meditation he receives an answer that satisfies him: "Behold, he whose soul is not upright in him shall fail, but the righteous shall live by his faith" (Habakkuk 2:4).

In Habakkuk 2:18–19 the powerlessness of idols is described, followed in verse 20 with the contrasting power of the living God: "But the Lord is in his holy temple; let all the earth keep silence before him." You will recognize this as the first sentence for the opening of Daily Morning and Evening Prayer in the Book of Common Prayer, pp. 3 and 21.

18

BY THE WATERS OF BABYLON

As WE HAVE SEEN, when Babylonia conquered Judah in 587 B.C., the so-called Babylonian Exile began. Some of the leading citizens had already been taken away in captivity in 598 B.C., but after the final downfall of Jerusalem, many more were deported. No longer was Israel a nation in a political sense, with capital, king, and all that goes with a separate government.

What effect did this have on the religion of the Israelites? Instead of causing the people to forget their ancestral faith, being carried away to a strange land caused them to re-think it. No longer able to have their religion centered in the Temple at Jerusalem, they made the happy discovery that God was with them even in Babylonia. They still had their history, their covenant, and now they also were able to establish synagogues where they could study, meet, and pray together, and they still had the religion of Moses as their guide.

The Exile lasted until Babylonia was succeeded by a new empire, that of Cyrus of Persia. When he conquered Babylon in 539 B.C., Cyrus permitted those Jews who wished to, to return to Palestine.

Several writings of the Old Testament belong to the period of the Exile.

Ezekiel

The prophet Ezekiel was taken to Babylonia in the 598 B.C. group of exiles. This shows that Ezekiel must have been con-

MAP 1

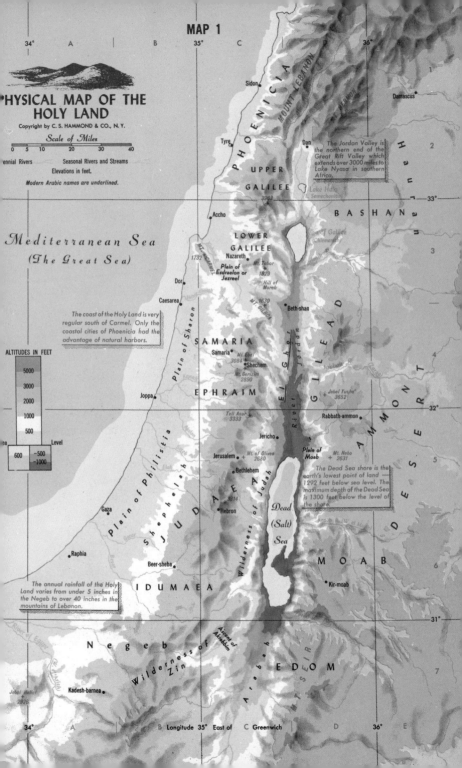

PHYSICAL MAP OF THE HOLY LAND

Copyright by C. S. HAMMOND & CO., N. Y.

Scale of Miles

0 5 10   20   30   40

ennial Rivers   Seasonal Rivers and Streams
            Elevations in feet.
    Modern Arabic names are underlined.

Mediterranean Sea
(The Great Sea)

ALTITUDES IN FEET

| 5000 |
| 3000 |
| 2000 |
| 1000 |
| 500 |
| Level |
| 600 | −500 −1000 |

The coast of the Holy Land is very
regular south of Carmel. Only the
coastal cities of Phoenicia had the
advantage of natural harbors.

The Jordan Valley is
the northern end of the
Great Rift Valley which
extends over 3000 miles to
Lake Nyasa in southern
Africa.

The Dead Sea shore is the
earth's lowest point of land —
1292 feet below sea level. The
maximum depth of the Dead Sea
is 1300 feet below the level of
the shore.

The annual rainfall of the Holy
Land varies from under 5 inches in
the Negeb to over 40 inches in the
mountains of Lebanon.

Sidon
Damascus
PHOENICIA
Tyre
MOUNT LEBANON
UPPER
GALILEE
Dan
Lake Huleh
Semechonitis
Accho
BASHAN
Lake of Galilee
Chinnereth
LOWER
GALILEE
Nazareth
Mt. Tabor
1929
Plain of
Esdraelon or
Jezreel
Hill of
Moreh
1732
1630
Dor
Beth-shan
GILEAD
Caesarea
Plain of Sharon
El Ghor
SAMARIA
Samaria
Mt. Ebal
3084
Shechem
Mt. Gerizim
2890
Jebel Yum'a
3652
Joppa
EPHRAIM
Tell Asur
3333
River Jordan
Rabbath-ammon
AMMON
Jericho
Jerusalem
Mt. of Olives
2680
Plain of
Moab
Mt. Nebo
2631
Bethlehem
3914
DESERT
Gaza
Hebron
Wilderness of Judah
Dead
(Salt)
Sea
Raphia
Kir-moab
MOAB
Beer-sheba
IDUMAEA
Negeb
Arabah
EDOM
MT. SEIR
Wilderness of Zin
Ascent of Akrabbim
Jebel Halal
Kadesh-barnea

34°   A   B   35°   C   36°   D   E
Longitude 35° East of Greenwich

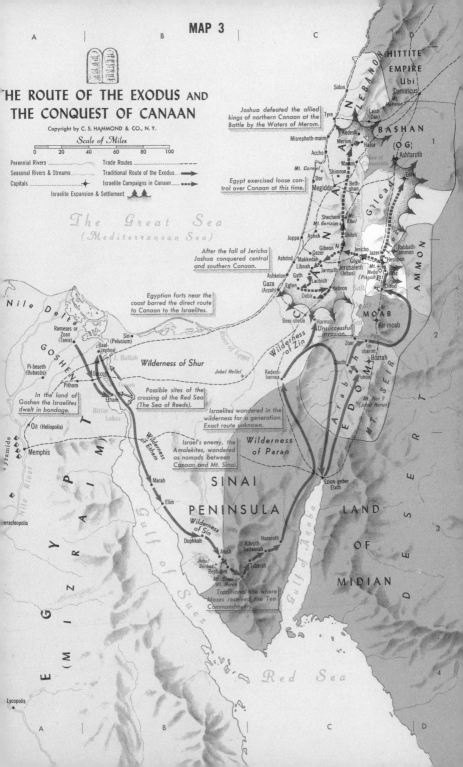

MAP 3

THE ROUTE OF THE EXODUS AND THE CONQUEST OF CANAAN

Copyright by C. S. HAMMOND & CO., N.Y.

Scale of Miles

0   20   40   60   80   100

Perennial Rivers .... Trade Routes ....
Seasonal Rivers & Streams .... Traditional Route of the Exodus →
Capitals .... Israelite Campaigns in Canaan ▶▶▶
Israelite Expansion & Settlement 🌲🌲

The Great Sea
(Mediterranean Sea)

HITTITE EMPIRE
Ubi
Damascus
Mt. Hermon

LEBANON

Sidon
Tyre
Laish (Dan)
Kedesh
BASHAN
Hazor
(OG)
Ashtaroth
Edrei

Joshua defeated the allied kings of northern Canaan at the Battle by the Waters of Merom.

Misrephoth-maim
Accho
Merom
Madon
Mt. Carmel
Shimron
Dor
Bethshan
Megiddo

Egypt exercised loose control over Canaan at this time.

Gilead

Shechem
Mt. Gerizim
Mt. Ebal
Shiloh
Joppa
Aphek

Rabbathammon

AMMON

After the fall of Jericho Joshua conquered central and southern Canaan.

Gibeon Ai
Gezer
Jericho
Jazer
Gilgal
Mt. Nebo
Pisgah
Heshbon
Ashdod
Makkedah
Jerusalem (Jebus)
Libnah
Jarmuth
Ashkelon
Gath
Lachish
Gaza (Azzah)
Eglon
Hebron
Debir
Jahaz
Dibon

Egyptian forts near the coast barred the direct route to Canaan to the Israelites.

MOAB
Ar
Kir-moab

Nile Delta

Rameses or Zoan (Tanis)
Baal-zephon
L. Ballah
GOSHEN
Sin (Pelusium)
Pi-beseth (Bubastis)
Pithom
Succoth
Etham

Wilderness of Shur

River of Egypt

Jebel Helal

Beer-sheba
Hormah
Unsuccessful invasion.
Zoar
Ije-abarim
Bozrah
Oboth
Punon
Mt. Hor? (Jebel Harun)

Kadesh-barnea

Wilderness of Zin

In the land of Goshen the Israelites dwelt in bondage.

Bitter Lakes

Possible sites of the crossing of the Red Sea (The Sea of Reeds).

On (Heliopolis)

Memphis

Israelites wandered in the wilderness for a generation. Exact route unknown.

Israel's enemy, the Amalekites, wandered as nomads between Canaan and Mt. Sinai.

Wilderness of Etham

Marah

Elim

Wilderness of Paran

SINAI PENINSULA

Ezion-geber Elath

LAND OF MIDIAN

Wilderness of Sin

Dophkah

Alush

Hazeroth

Kibroth-hattaavah

Rephidim
Jebel Serbal
Mt. Sinai?
Mt. Horeb

Taberah

Traditional site where Moses received the Ten Commandments.

Gulf of Suez

Gulf of Aqaba

DESERT

Red Sea

Lycopolis

Heracleopolis

Pyramids

Nile River

EGYPT (MIZRAIM)

EDOM

Mt. SEIR

Arabah

Salt Sea

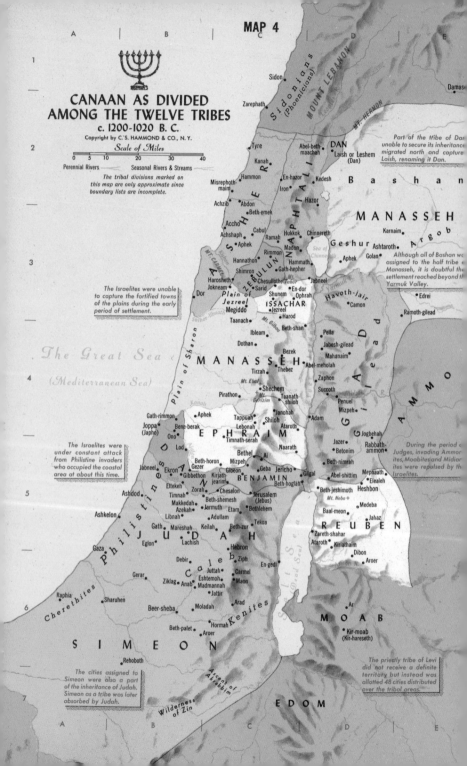

MAP 5

THE KINGDOMS OF ISRAEL AND JUDAH
c. 925-842 B.C.

Copyright by C. S. HAMMOND & CO., N. Y.

Scale of Miles

0 5 10 20 30 40

Perennial Rivers ....

Seasonal Rivers & Streams

Capitals ....

Egyptian & Syrian Attacks ⟶

Elijah took refuge in Zarephath and brought back to life the widow's son.

In the reign of Baasha the cities of northern Israel were raided by the King of Damascus in league with Asa, King of Judah.

Aram waged almost constant war against Israel. The Syrians were held in check by Ahab until his death in battle at Ramoth-gilead.

Elijah challenged the prophets of Baal at Mt. Carmel.

The introduction of Phoenician cults following the marriage of Ahab with Jezebel caused violent reactions in Israel that eventually wiped out the house of Omri.

Samaria, fortress capital of Israel was built by Omri c. 870 B.C.

Moab was ruled as a vassal kingdom during the Omri dynasty. The Dibon stele commemorates the victory of Mesha, King of Moab, over Israel and the return of Moabite independence.

Shishak (Sheshonk), Egyptian Pharaoh, raided the divided kingdoms, plundering Jerusalem c. 925 B.C.

During the reign of Jehosophat Judah regained control over Edom.

The Great Sea
(Mediterranean Sea)

MOUNT LEBANON

MT. HERMON

PHOENICIA

Sidon
Zarephath
Tyre
Ijon
Abel-beth-maachah
Dan
Kedesh
Hazor
Accho
Cabul
Chinnereth
Sea of Chinnereth
Hammath
Mt. Tabor

Damascus
Abana R.
A r a m a e a n s
A S S Y R I A N S
GESHUR
Karnaim
Ashtaroth
Aphek
Bashan
Edrei
Ramoth-gilead

Dor
Megiddo
Taanach
Dothan
MT. CARMEL
Plain of Jezreel
Shunem
Jezreel
Ibleam
Beth-shan
Jabesh-gilead
Tishbe
Mahanaim
Havoth-jair

Sochoh
Samaria
Mt. Ebal
Tirzah
Abel-meholah
Shechem
Mt. Gerizim
Janohah
Shiloh
Penuel
GILEAD
Jabbok R.

Aphek
Plain of Sharon
Joppa
Jeshanah
Zemaraim
Lod
Beth-horon
Bethel
Aijalon
Mizpeh
Ramah
Gezer
Geba
Jericho
Gilgal
AMMON
Rabbath-ammon

Jabneel
Ekron
Gibbethon
Zorah
Beth-shemesh
Timnah
Jerusalem
Azekah
Bethlehem
Ashdod
Shoco
Etam
Tekoa
Libnah
Adullam
Gath
Mareshah
Beth-zur
Lachish
Hebron
Adoraim
Debir
Ashkelon
Ziph
En-gedi
Gaza
PHILISTIA
JUDAH
Wilderness of Judah
Elealeh
Heshbon
Mt. Nebo
Medeba
Baal-meon
Jahaz
Ataroth
Dibon
Aroer
M O A B
Ar
Kir-moab (Kir-haresheth)

Gerar
Ziklag
Raphia
Beer-sheba
Salt (Dead) Sea
Valley of Salt

EDOM

I S R A E L

MAP 6

GREAT EMPIRES OF THE SIXTH CENTURY B.C.

Copyright by C. S. HAMMOND & CO., N.Y.

Scale of Miles

0 100 200 300 400 500

Capitals
Limit of the Persian Empire c. 500 B.C.
Persian Royal Road
Red Sea-Nile Canal Built by Darius I

MEDIAN EMPIRE (625–550 B.C.)

PERSIAN EMPIRE

NEW BABYLONIAN EMPIRE (625–539 B.C.)

The Persians under Cyrus the Great overthrew the Medes, conquered Lydia and Babylonia, to fulfill the prophecy of Daniel.

The Edict of Cyrus (538 B.C.) allowed the Jews to return to their homeland.

The rise of the New Babylonian (Chaldean) Empire brought an end to the Kingdom of Judah and exile of her people.

Dorius I extended the Persian Empire into Europe. Attempts to subjugate Greece by Dorius I and Xerxes I failed by the Greek won at Marathon and Salamis.

Pharaoh Necho of Judah but was later driven defeated Josiah, out of Palestine after being defeated by Nebuchadnezzar at Carchemish (605 B.C.).

Egypt came under Persian rule after Cambyses defeated Psamtik III at Pelusium in 525 B.C.

Seas and regions

Arabian Sea
Caspian Sea (Mare Hyrcanium)
Aral Sea
Black Sea (Pontus Euxinus)
Mediterranean Sea
Red Sea
Persian Gulf

Peoples and regions

SCYTHIANS
Massagetae (Saka Scythians)
INDIA
SOGDIANA
CHORASMIA
MARGIANA
BACTRIA
ARIA
ARACHOSIA
GEDROSIA (MAKA)
CARMANIA
PERSIS
PARTHIA
HYRCANIA
MEDIAN EMPIRE
ARMENIA
CAPPADOCIA
PAPHLAGONIA
KINGDOM OF LYDIA (670–546 B.C.)
THRACE
MACEDONIA
EPIRUS
ILLYRIA
GREECE
CRETE
CYPRUS
ASSYRIA
NEW
ARABIA
JUDAH
KINGDOM OF EGYPT (26th DYNASTY 663–525 B.C.)
LIBYANS
ETHIOPIA (CUSH)
Dahae
Cadusii
COLCHIS
LYCIA
ELAM
SUSIANA
UTIANS
PACTYANS
PARICANIANS
SARANGIANS
DRANGIANA

Cities and places

Maracanda (Samarkand)
Bactra
Bagae
Taxila
Pattala
Gandara
Ecbatana (Achmetha)
Behistun
Rhagae
Amadai
Aspadana
Pasargadae
Persepolis
Susa (Shushan)
Opis
Babylon
Sippar
Nippur
Erech
Ur
Harran
Tadmor
Damascus
Byblos
Sidon
Tyre
Megiddo
Jerusalem
Gaza
Pelusium
Tahpanhes
Sais
Naucratis
On
Memphis (Noph)
Thebes (No)
Pathros
Syene (Elephantine)
Ammonium
Cyrene
Barca
Elath
Tarsus
Arvad
Sinope
Pteria
Ancyra
Trapezus
Phasis
Ninus (Nineveh)
Nicaea
Pessinus
Sardis
Miletus
Ephesus
Athens
Sparta
Thermopylae
Marathon
Salamis
Byzantium
Chalcedon
Apollonia
Olbia
Chersonesus
Panticapaeum
Rhodes

Tigris R.
Present shoreline

MAP 7

PALESTINE IN THE TIME OF CHRIST

Copyright by C. S. HAMMOND & CO., N. Y.

Scale of Miles

0 5 10   20   30   40

Perennial Rivers ....
Seasonal Rivers & Streams
Capitals ....
Roads & Trade Routes _____

Tetrarchy of Lysanias
Tetrarchy of Philip
Tetrarchy of Herod Antipas
Territory under Roman procurator

Areas tributary to Salome
Decapolis *
Independent *
Roman province of Syria

Cities of the Decapolis ......

* The Decapolis and Ascalon retained their independence under the Roman governor of the province of Syria.

Archelaus, upon Herod's death, became ruler of Judaea, Samaria and Idumaea. His reign lasted until 6 A.D. when he was removed and exiled. His territory then was placed under a Roman procurator.

Salome, Herod's sister, was given Jamnia, Azotus and Phasaelis. They, in turn, passed to Livia, wife of Augustus and then to Emperor Tiberius.

ABILENE
Abila
Damascus

Sidon

Sarepta (Zarephath)

Tyre

PANIAS
Dan · Caesarea Philippi
ULATHA
Lake Semechonitis

Cadasa (Kedesh)
Gischala
Horns of Hattin (Kurūn Hattin) is a possible site of the Sermon on the Mount.

Ladder of Tyre

Ptolemais (Accho)

Jotapata
Cana
GALILEE
Sepphoris
Nazareth

Chorazin
Bethsaida (Julias)
Capernaum
Magdala (Dalmanutha) Tabgha
Horns of Hattin
Tiberias
Philoteria
Mt. Tabor

Sea of Galilee

GAULANITIS
BATANAEA

TRACHONITIS
BASHAN
Raphana

Seleucia
Gamala
Hippos
Gergesa
Dion
AURANITIS
Abila
Gadara
Capitolias
Edrei

Plain of Esdraelon
Nain

Dora

The Great Sea

(Mediterranean Sea)

Caesarea
Residence of Roman procurators.

En-gannim (Ginaea)
Scythopolis (Beth-shan)
Bethabara
Pella
DECAPOLIS

SAMARIA
Samaria (Sebaste)
Mt. Ebal
Shechem
Sychar
Mt. Gerizim
Jacob's Well
Amathus
Gerasa

GILEAD

Apollonia
Antipatris

Joppa
Arimathaea (Ramathaim)
Lydda (Diospolis)
Gezer (Gazara)
Ramah
Jamnia
Ekron
Nicopolis (Emmaus)
Emmaus
Azotus (Ashdod)
Ascalon

Gaza

Gerar

Raphia

Phasaelis
Archelais
Gophna
Bethel
Ephraim
Jericho
Mt. of Olives
Jerusalem
Bethany
Bethlehem

PERAEA
Beth-nimrah
Julias (Livias, Beth-haram)
Philadelphia (Rabbath-ammon)
Heshbon

Khirbet Qumran
The Dead Sea Scrolls were found in a cave here; also the ruins of an Essene monastery.

Herodium
JUDAEA
Mareshah (Marisa)
Hebron
Ziph
Juttah
Carmel
En-gedi
Masada

Wilderness of Judah

Sea of Dead Sea (L. Asphaltitis)

Callirhoe
Machaerus
Dibon

Here John the Baptist was imprisoned and beheaded by order of Herod Antipas.

IDUMAEA
Beersheba

Rabbath Moab (Areopolis, Rabba)

Kir-moab (Kir-haresheth)

NABATAEANS

ARABIA

PHOENICIA
MOUNT LEBANON
MT. HERMON
ITURAEA
Mt. Carmel
Plain of Sharon
River Jordan

MAP 8

Rome · Ortona
Three Taverns
Appii
Forum
Puteoli · Neapolis · Beneventum
Buxentum · Tarentum · Anxa
ITALY · Brundisium

ILLYRICUM
(DALMATIA)
Scodra
Dyrrhachium
MACEDONIA
Berea
EPIRUS
Corcyra · Nicopolis
Larisa
ACHAIA
Corinth · Athens
Cenchrea
(GREECE)
Sparta

Tyrrhenian
Sea

Messana
SICILY · Rhegium
Agrigentum · Syracuse

MELITA
(MALTA)

MOESIA
THRACE
Mesembria
Philippi · Neapolis
Amphipolis
Apollonia
Thessalonica
SAMOTHRACE
Byzantium
Nicomedia
Nicaea
BITHYNIA
Germanicopolis
Heraclea
Pontica
Amastris
Amasia
Zela
PAPHLAGONIA
PONTU
Sinope
Amisus

Troas · Adramyttium
Assos · Mysia
LESBOS
Mitylene · Pergamum
Thyatira
Sardis
Smyrna · Lydia
CHIOS · Ephesus
SAMOS
Philadelphia
Hierapolis
Laodicea
Miletus · Colossae
Trogyllium · Caria
COOS · Cnidus
Xanthus
RHODES · Patara
Phenice · Cnossus
CRETE · Lasea
CLAUDA
C. Salmone
Cydonia

Dorylaeum
ASIA
GALATIA
Pessinus
Ancyra
Tavium
Caesarea
Mazaca
CAPPADOCI
Starting point
of 1st & 2nd
Antioch
Lycaonia
Iconium · Tyana
Lystra
Derbe · CILICIA
PISIDIA
PAMPHYLIA
Perga · Attalia
LYCIA · Selinus
Myra · Tarsus
Seleucia

CYPRUS
Salamis
Paphos

Phoenicia
Damascu
Sidon
Tyre
Ptolemais

Caesarea
Joppa · Jerusalem
Gaza · Judaea
Limit of Roman Em

The Great

In the past it was believed that
Paul visited the Galatian cities of
Pessinus, Ancyra and Tavium.
Modern scholars doubt this.

ST. PAUL'S FIRST AND
SECOND JOURNEYS
Copyright by C. S. HAMMOND & CO., N. Y.

Scale of Miles
0 50 100   200   300
First Journey   Second Journey

Catabathmus
Marmarica · Paraetonium
Libya
PHAROS
Alexandria
EGYPT
Memphis · Heliopolis
Pelusium
ARABIA

(Mediterranean) Sea

MAP 9

Rome · Ortona
Three Taverns
Appii
Forum
Puteoli · Neapolis · Beneventum
Buxentum · Tarentum · Anxa
ITALY · Brundisium

ILLYRICUM
(DALMATIA)
Scodra
Dyrrhachium
MACEDONIA
Berea
EPIRUS
Corcyra · Nicopolis
Larisa
ACHAIA
Corinth · Athens
Cenchrea
(GREECE)
Sparta

Tyrrhenian
Sea

Messana
SICILY · Rhegium
Agrigentum · Syracuse

MELITA
(MALTA)

MOESIA
THRACE
Mesembria
Philippi · Neapolis
Amphipolis
Apollonia
Thessalonica
SAMOTHRACE
Byzantium
Nicomedia
Nicaea
BITHYNIA
Germanicopolis
Heraclea
Pontica
Amastris
Amasia
Zela
PAPHLAGONIA
PONTU
Sinope
Amisus

Troas · Adramyttium
Assos · Mysia
LESBOS
Mitylene · Pergamum
Thyatira
Smyrna · Lydia
Sardis
CHIOS · Ephesus
SAMOS
Philadelphia
Hierapolis
Laodicea
Miletus · Colossae
Trogyllium
COOS · Cnidus
Xanthus
RHODES · Patara
Phenice · Cnossus
CRETE · Lasea
CLAUDA
C. Salmone
Cydonia

Dorylaeum
ASIA
GALATIA
Pessinus
Ancyra
Tavium
Caesarea
Mazaca
CAPPADOCI
Antioch
Lycaonia
Iconium · Tyana
Lystra
Derbe
PISIDIA
Starting
point of
3rd journe
PAMPHYLIA
Perga · Attalia
LYCIA · Selinus
Myra · Tarsus
Seleucia
Antioch

CYPRUS
Salamis
Paphos

Phoenicia
Sidon
Tyre
Ptolemais

Caesarea
Joppa · Jerusalem
Gaza · Judaea
Limit of Roman Em

An ancient tradition states that
Paul traveled extensively throughout the Mediterranean world after
his journey to Rome.

Starting point of
journey to Rome

ST. PAUL'S THIRD JOURNEY
AND
HIS JOURNEY TO ROME
Copyright by C. S. HAMMOND & CO., N. Y.

Scale of Miles
0 50 100   200   300
Third Journey   Journey to Rome

Catabathmus
Marmarica · Paraetonium
Libya
PHAROS
Alexandria
EGYPT
Memphis · Heliopolis
Pelusium
ARABIA

The Great (Mediterranean) Sea

sidered one of the more important or "substantial" citizens. Only the "cream of the crop" were taken in the first deportation, for Nebuchadnezzar had wanted to leave behind the poorer, less prominent people. Ezekiel apparently had settled at a place called Tel-abib. By the banks of the river Chebar he had his call to become a prophet; God had not ceased raising up prophets now that many of the people were no longer in Palestine.

His vision at the beginning of his career is set forth in the first two chapters of the book that has his name. Like other prophets before him, he was unable to imagine that he was called of God for this work. We read that the vision was so overpowering that he fell upon his face, but immediately the word of the Lord came to him, "Son of man, stand upon your feet, and I will speak with you" (Ezekiel 2:1). Then he received his commission to go to a rebellious people and say to them, "Thus says the Lord God" (Ezekiel 2:4).

One set of prophecies in the book of Ezekiel was written before the downfall of Jerusalem in 587 (Chapters 1–24). He, like Jeremiah, was sure that the city would be completely ruined as would be surrounding nations. Remember, he was writing for exiles who were living in the hope that the Babylonian power would be weakened so that Judah could be restored once more to power. That he saw to be a hopeless expectation.

After the destruction of Jerusalem in 587, Ezekiel began to stress another note (Chapters 33–39). Now he *did* talk in terms of hope. In Chapter 37 there is the famous story of the dry bones that came alive again when the Spirit of the Lord God breathed upon them.

> Then he said to me, "Son of man, these bones are the whole house of Israel. Behold, they say, 'Our bones are dried up, and our hope is lost; we are clean cut off.' Therefore prophesy, and say to them, Thus says the Lord God: "Behold, I

will open your graves, and raise you from your graves, O my
people; and I will bring you home into the land of Israel. . . .
And I will put my Spirit within you, and you shall live, and
I will place you in your own land; then you shall know that
I, the Lord, have spoken, and I have done it, says the Lord"
(Ezekiel 37:11–14).

That is a way of saying that God will restore them because of
the covenant of old if they remain faithful to His Spirit.

The people will have this renewal in so far as they receive
the new heart that God wants them to have. "A new heart I
will give you, and a new spirit I will put within you; and
I will take out of your flesh the heart of stone and give you
a heart of flesh" (Ezekiel 36:26). He predicted that Jerusalem would rise a great new city and that there would be a
new Temple for a new united kingdom. It did not turn out
that way because Jerusalem, even when rebuilt, never regained its former glory, and the people of north and south
intensely disliked one another. Those descended from the
Israelites who had remained in Israel came to be known as
Samaritans.

The Second Isaiah

When we discussed the book of Isaiah, we said that Chapters
40–55 are not from Isaiah himself but belong to the period of
the Exile. This is known from the fact that the situation
described by the author is entirely different from the days
before the fall of Jerusalem. In this account, the people are
living in exile, Babylonia is the chief power among the nations, and Cyrus of Persia is praised as the person who will be
the Lord's shepherd, who will fulfill the Lord's purpose,
"saying of Jerusalem, 'She shall be built,' and of the temple,
'Your foundation shall be laid' " (Isaiah 44:28). It is prob-
able that Chapters 56–66 are by a still later writer whom the
scholars refer to as the Third Isaiah. The author of the second

section of the book of Isaiah is trying to comfort the people.
They had had their punishment. The Lord would restore
them to their homeland in due time.

> Comfort, comfort my people,
>   says your God.
> Speak tenderly to Jerusalem,
>   and cry to her
> that her warfare is ended,
>   that her iniquity is pardoned,
> that she has received from the Lord's hand
>   double for all her sins (Isaiah 40:1–2).

Anyone who reads the Second Isaiah carefully will be impressed by the passages in which the writer refers to "the
servant." These are found in Chapters 42, 49, 50, 52, and 53.
It is not known for sure whether an individual (the Messiah)
is referred to or Israel as a redeeming people. These are passages of great power and spiritual understanding. God's
servant will be one who suffers for the sins of many. Jesus
Christ must certainly have been familiar with this material
and pondered its meaning for His own ministry. He may have
found in it a pattern for His own life. In any event, looking
back at Christ, the Christian people always have thought
of Him as the fulfillment of the suffering servant portrayed
by the Second Isaiah:

> He was despised and rejected by men;
>   a man of sorrows, and acquainted with grief. . . .
> Surely he has borne our griefs
>   and carried our sorrows; . . .
>   and with his stripes we are healed.
> All we like sheep have gone astray;
>   we have turned every one to his own way;
> and the Lord has laid on him the iniquity of us all
>   (Isaiah 53:3–6).

Sections of the writing of the Second and Third Isaiah are

appointed to be read as the Epistle on several Sundays of the year during Holy Communion: the Second Sunday after Christmas (Isaiah 61:1–3; The Book of Common Prayer, p. 106f.), the Monday before Easter (Isaiah 63, p. 138f.), St. John Baptist, June 24 (Isaiah 40:1–11, p. 242f.).

19

RETURN AND REBUILDING

THE SECOND ISAIAH had hailed Cyrus of Persia as the one anointed of God to liberate the people of Israel from Babylonia. There is in existence a clay barrel from the time of the Persian period called the "Cyrus Cylinder." On this there is an inscription telling about Cyrus' conquering of Babylon. There it is said that Marduk, the god of Babylon, grew angry with the Babylonian ruler. Looking through all countries for a righteous ruler, he chose Cyrus of Persia to be the ruler of the world.

Cyrus was apparently welcomed not only by the Israelites in Babylonia but also by the Babylonians themselves, for he had a reputation of being a generous and lenient ruler. He proved that he was a good statesman in that he permitted the people to keep their particular customs and worship their own gods.

The people of Israel were to benefit from this policy of Cyrus'. In 538 B.C. he issued an edict which contained three things of importance to the Jews: (1) they were permitted to return to Palestine; (2) the Temple was to be rebuilt, with money being contributed by the Persian government; (3) the sacred vessels that Nebuchadnezzar had taken from the Temple were to be returned.

Cyrus appointed a man named Sheshbazzar to be in charge of the resettlement in Palestine. He served for only a short time, after which Zerubbabel took over. The important thing about these men is that they continued the line of David, being descendants in the royal family.

The prophet's dreams of a glorious restoration of Israel's former status did not materialize. For one thing, not everyone wanted to return. Many had found life in Babylonia not so bad; they had prospered to a certain extent and decided to stay on. Those who did go back found that their lot was not an easy one. How many returned? In Ezra 2 a listing of the returned exiles totals around 50,000, but this is based on a much later census. They did not all come back at once, but trickled in for several generations. The whole region around Jerusalem was still desolate, and those who returned faced a huge task of rebuilding with scant resources.

Another problem they faced was the need to get along with the people who were now dwelling in the land, who naturally were none too eager to see the competition for land and food which the returned settlers would cause. The Samaritans in the north, who considered themselves faithful followers of the Law of Moses, at first wanted to help in rebuilding the Temple, but Zerubbabel refused to let them. Later the Samaritans did all they could to interfere with the Temple's rebuilding, for they thought of it as a sign of Jewish national power.

Haggai and Zechariah

For about twenty years nothing much was accomplished on the rebuilding of the Temple except that the foundations of the building were laid. The difficulties were simply too great to be overcome.

Two prophets arose at this time to spur on the work of rebuilding. We have their books in the Old Testament. One of them is Haggai. His brief writing contains only two chapters. This is the way he begins his appeal:

"Thus says the Lord of hosts: This people say the time has not yet come to rebuild the house of the Lord." Then the word of the Lord came by Haggai the prophet, "Is it a time for you yourselves to dwell in your paneled houses, while this house lies in ruins? Now therefore thus says the Lord of hosts: Consider how you have fared. You have sown much, and harvested little; you eat, but you never have enough; you drink, but you never have your fill; you clothe yourselves, but no one is warm; and he who earns wages earns wages to put them into a bag with holes" (Haggai 1:2–6).

Why is this so? Everyone is busy with his own selfish concerns and neglects the house of the Lord! They worked hard for a month, but then they felt discouraged when they saw that the new Temple was going to be much smaller and plainer than the great one that had been destroyed. Haggai urged them on, saying "The latter splendor of this house shall be greater than the former . . . and in this place I will give prosperity, says the Lord of hosts" (Haggai 2:9).

Zechariah's writing deals with the same task of rebuilding. He is interested in the total rebuilding of the city of Jerusalem, including the Temple, but including much more as well, because he is strongly nationalistic. He looks forward to the time when the Davidic king and the High Priest will once again rule under the protection of the Lord. Evidently the writer is thinking of Zerubbabel as the one who will continue the line of David, a kind of messianic king, when he says:

"Thus says the Lord of hosts, 'Behold the man whose name is the Branch; for he shall grow up in his place, and he shall build the temple of the Lord. It is he who shall build the temple of the Lord, and shall bear royal honor, and shall sit and rule upon his throne. And there shall be a priest by his throne, and peaceful understanding shall be between them both'" (Zechariah 6:12–13).

The last six chapters of the book of Zechariah were written about three hundred years later than Zechariah himself.

The Chronicler

During the period after the Exile, a writer (or writers) whose name (or names) is completely unknown—so we shall call him (or them) "the Chronicler"—set down a history of Israel from the time of Saul through the time just before 400 B.C. The writer seems to have been a member of the priestly order named Levites, who served at the Temple, for the whole history is edited in such a way as to stress the life of Israel as a worshipping body, a holy nation, centered in the Jerusalem Temple.

There are four books in our Bible that are the Chronicler's work: I and II Chronicles, Ezra, and Nehemiah. Originally Ezra and Nehemiah were one writing, the second part of the history. The Chronicles cover the same territory as II Samuel and the two books of Kings. One way to look at the two different sets of historical material is to say that the Samuel and Kings stories tend to be more inclusive. They tell both the good and bad points about David, for example. The Chronicler portrays David's house as perfectly as the writer could make it appear, and the bad is seldom referred to.

The books of Ezra and Nehemiah deal with the rebuilding of the nation. Ezra is called "the father of Judaism" (Israel's religion after the Exile), for he was responsible for bringing back with him the book of the Law of Moses. He began a reconstruction of the religious life of the people based on a strict interpretation of the five books of Moses, the Pentateuch. Nehemiah became the governor of Jerusalem in 445 B.C. He rebuilt the city walls, a difficult task since the Samaritans were very much opposed to the new Jewish nationalism and did everything in their power to interrupt the work. Nehemiah, like Ezra, insisted on making a sharp difference between Jew and Gentile. A good Jew was born into a family that could trace itself back to a Jewish ancestor. Also, a good

Jew, he insisted, was one who lived by the Law and took the Temple worship seriously. This strict Judaism was an effort to recapture the religious past of Israel in a time when the religious life of the people had been at a low ebb.

20

LIFE IN THE NEW ISRAEL

THERE ARE SEVERAL short writings in the Old Testament which give little pictures of conditions in Palestine during the period after the Exile.

Three of these were probably written before the coming of Nehemiah as governor, although it is difficult for the scholars to know the exact dates of their writing.

Obadiah

Obadiah consists of twenty-one verses only, one of the shortest books in the Bible. It is a protest against the nation of Edom. After the fall of Jerusalem, this neighboring country had taken a part of Judah. There had been a number of conflicts between the people of Israel and the people of Edom from way back when the Israelites were first getting settled in Canaan. The Edomites, you will remember, were associated with the name of Esau, Jacob's twin brother. Although they were traditional enemies of Israel, their seizure of land seemed all the worse because both peoples did not have a common ancestry.

Obadiah definitely does not like the Edomites. He sets down a great many things that he does not like about them, calling to mind many things they have done that he says they should not have done. For example:

> You should not have entered the gate of my people
> in the day of his calamity;

you should not have gloated over his disaster
  in the day of his calamity;
you should not have looted his goods
  in the day of his calamity (Obadiah 13).

They will be punished, he says, in the coming Day of the Lord: "As you have done, it shall be done to you, your deeds shall return on your own head" (Obadiah 15).

Malachi

The book that is placed last in our Old Testament was written even before the arrival of Nehemiah as governor. The Temple had been completed. The writer is unhappy over the low grade of religious living and worship which the people were showing. They were offering imperfect animals for sacrifices; they were divorcing their wives to marry foreigners; they were saying it was no use to worship God when evildoers seemed to prosper more. Against all these things the writer protests. God will not be deceived; He knows who are true in their service of Him and has their names written in "a book of remembrance" (Malachi 3:16). The word "Malachi" means "My Messenger" and may not be the name of one person but rather the title for a prophet. One great verse in Malachi (1:11) is an opening Sentence in Morning Prayer, in the Book of Common Prayer (p. 4).

Joel

From the book of Joel (2:13) comes another often-used opening Sentence in Morning Prayer, the one designated for Lent:

Rend your heart, and not your garments, and turn unto the Lord your God: for he is gracious and merciful, slow to anger, and of great kindness, and repenteth him of the evil (The Book of Common Prayer, p. 4).

Like Obadiah, the date of Joel is uncertain. Most of the
other prophets had pointed to some military or political danger as a warning to the people to repent of their evil ways
and turn unto the Lord. With Joel, however, it was something else. There had been a famine and on top of that a great
plague of locusts had descended on the country, eating up all
the foliage:

> For a nation has come up against my land,
>   powerful and without number;
> its teeth are lions' teeth,
>   and it has the fangs of a lioness.
> It has laid waste my vines,
>   and splintered my fig trees;
> it has stripped off their bark and thrown it down;
>   their branches are made white (Joel 1:6–7).

The prophet sees the attack on the locusts as a sign of the
coming Day of the Lord. What should the people do? He
calls them to repent: "For the day of the Lord is great and
very terrible; who can endure it?" (Joel 2:11).

He goes on to promise that after the judgment, the Lord
will restore their health and prosperity. The foliage will blos-
som and bear fruit once again. "You shall know that I am in
the midst of Israel, and that I, the Lord, am your God and
there is none else" (Joel 2:27).

Protests against Nationalism

After Ezra's and Nehemiah's reforms, when a great deal of
stress was being put on nationalism, there were two writers
who protested against a too narrow view of Jewish life.

One of these is in the form of a short novel, the book of
Ruth. It was written at this period, but the author makes its
setting the days of the ancient tribal period when the judges
ruled. This is done very much as a modern writer might
choose to describe a present-day situation by telling a story

that has its setting back in the days of the American colonies in the South or in New England. This approach was used in a particularly skillful fashion by the author of Ruth, for people reading it got the lesson without having it pointed out to them in so many words as the prophets were always doing. What the author tries to do in telling this story about Ruth and Boaz is to show that a non-Jew (Ruth was a Moabitess) became the ancestor of King David, who was regarded as the greatest man in Jewish history. He is saying, in other words, that the Jews should not think that having the right ancestor was the final thing. God worked out His purpose even through a marriage between a Jew and a Moabitess, a mixed marriage of the type Ezra and Nehemiah strongly opposed.

Another protest came in the book of Jonah. This, like Ruth, is in story form, although it is more like a short, short story than a novelette. It is a deliberately fantastic tale, so written that it entertains as well as instructs us. It tells about Jonah, a preacher-prophet who is commanded by the Lord to go to Nineveh, capital of Assyria. Now, being a devout Jew who shared in the intense hatred for Assyria that most of his fellow men felt, Jonah could not think of going there to preach. So he took a ship in the other direction, heading for Tarshish. During a great storm, the sailors decided to draw lots to see who on board was responsible for the displeasure of God, who would permit such a storm to rage. Jonah was the man chosen, and he was thrown overboard in order to quiet the storm. Instead of drowning, the story says that Jonah was swallowed by "a great fish" (note—it does not say a whale) which preserved the prophet until he was spat out on dry land.

Jonah encountered a second time the command to go to Nineveh. This time he went, proclaiming that in forty days Nineveh would be overthrown. The people believed his words and repented; even the king did, proclaiming a fast.

Imagine Israel's greatest enemy being forgiven and spared by God! This made Jonah very angry indeed. It was not until he had an interesting and strange experience under a large shade tree (which the sun dried up so that Jonah felt pity toward the plant) that he understood the message God had been conveying:

> You pity the plant. . . . And should not I [the Lord] pity Nineveh, that great city, in which there are more than a hundred and twenty thousand persons who do not know their right hand from their left, and also much cattle? (Jonah 4:10–11).

In both Ruth and Jonah we see an understanding of God that went beyond mere nationalism. It is the insight that the Second Isaiah had had: "I am the Lord, who made all things" (Isaiah 44:24).

21

NEW PROBLEMS

THE HEBREW BIBLE was divided, as we mentioned before, into three great sections: (1) The Law (Torah); (2) The Prophets; and (3) The Writings.

We come now to a consideration of the so-called Writings. As a matter of fact, we have already taken up several books which are classified under Writings because they seemed better suited to be looked at in connection with other books of the periods being discussed. The Hebrew Bible includes these among the Writings: Ezra-Nehemiah, I and II Chronicles, Lamentations, and Ruth. Since we have referred to these already, we shall not repeat them in this section. All the other Writings we shall look at next.

Esther

Jonah's internationalism is very different from that of another nationalistic writing, the book of Esther. It, too, is a novel. This book is associated with the Jewish festival of Purim, an annual time of rejoicing, based on the remembrance of the events which are supposedly written up in the book.

Esther is a Jewess who becomes the wife of Xerxes. Two of the characters have a personal quarrel: Mordecai, a cousin of Esther's, and Haman, the grand vizier to the Persian king. Mordecai, a Jew proud of his people, refuses to show special courtesies demanded by Haman. Haman complains to the king, who orders that there shall be a wholesale massacre of the Jews on a certain day. Mordecai persuades Esther that she has a responsibility to her people to see the king although it was forbidden anyone—even a wife—to see the king unless he sent for one. Mordecai says to her: "Who knows whether you have not come to the kingdom for such a time as this?" (Esther 4:14). Esther very cleverly persuades the king during two dinners which she serves to him and Haman. It is a highly dramatic situation that comes to a climax in Chapter 7. You will enjoy reading it for yourself. We need only say that the queen's petition that her people be saved was granted, and Haman lost his life instead.

The rabbis who drew up the final canon (official list) of the Jewish Bible at the Council of Jamnia about the year A.D. 90 debated whether to include Esther in the canon. There is no specific religious purpose in the writing (the name of God is not mentioned in it). Because of its highly nationalistic nature, which might easily be taken wrongly by non-Jewish readers, it was thought to be questionable. Yet it was so popular a book in connection with Purim that they kept it.

The Maccabees

After the Persians came the Greeks as world leaders. As the Persians had spread westward, they came into conflict with the Greeks. It was not many years until the tide had turned, and the Greeks were pursuing the Persians. By 326 B.C. the Greek armies under the general Alexander the Great had reached the Indus River in what is today called Pakistan.

Alexander was not merely a great military man, he was also a great believer in the Greek civilization. Wherever his armies went, they carried with them Greek ideas about architecture, philosophy, art, and sports. Unfortunately, he died at the age of thirty-two. His empire was cut up into sections, ruled by his generals. Palestine was now under the influence of these Greek ways of life. The Greek word for Greece was *Hellas*. The movement which spread Greek ideas around the continents was called Hellenism.

Finally an extreme Hellenist came to be the ruler of that part of the empire which included Palestine. His name was Antiochus Epiphanes. He actually came to think of himself as a god and called himself Zeus-*made-manifest,* which is what Epiphanes means, Zeus being the chief Greek god. Everyone in the kingdom had to recognize him as a god.

This was a sore point with the Jews, for to them there could be no god but the true God of Israel. The ruler became hated, also, because in order to get money he levied big taxes on the people. He even went to the extent of appointing as High Priest in Palestine a man who offered a large sum of money for the honor.

When a rival who had wanted to be High Priest started riots in Jerusalem, Antiochus came to the city with his army. The Temple was plundered. Things got even worse. Orders were issued that the whole Jewish life should be Hellenized. For example, it was forbidden the Jews to keep the Sabbath or to have copies of the Torah. An altar to Zeus was set up in the Temple court. Soldiers patrolled the country to see that the new laws were carried out.

All of this led to a revolt led by Mattathias, a priest in a small town twenty miles from Jerusalem. He refused to make a sacrifice in honor of the Emperor and killed those who commanded him to do so. Mattathias and five sons went to the hill country where they formed a kind of guerilla army. The most famous of the sons was Judas, who carried on after Mattathias' death in 166 B.C. They called Judas *Maccabeus,* meaning *hammer.* Judas' army won a victory over Antiochus' troops on December 25, 165 B.C. The altar of Zeus was removed from the Temple court. Ever since, the Jews have celebrated that event and the re-consecration of the Temple in the festival of Hanukkah.

The Maccabees continued their revolt for some years afterward. The Jews had about a hundred years' freedom until Rome took over in A.D. 63. Two books of the Apocrypha, I and II Maccabees, tell of this period in Jewish history.

Daniel

The book of Daniel comes out of this period during which the Jews revolted against the Greek ways forced upon them.

The writer set his work in the time of the Babylonian Exile, Daniel being a character mentioned briefly in Ezekiel 14 and 28. Actually, he was writing about the history of the Exile in order to point up lessons for the guidance of the Jews in the period of the Greek supremacy. Stories are told of faithful Jews who refused to give up their loyalty to the God of Israel even when persecuted, like the three young men who were thrown into a fiery furnace where they were protected by angels.

These stories are found in the first six chapters. The last six chapters give a series of visions which Daniel is said to have seen. This is apocalyptic writing (referring to final things, the last days) of the type we have seen also in Zechariah. One after another Daniel saw the rise and fall of powerful kingdoms: the Babylonians, the Medes, the Persians, and the Greeks. In Chapter 11 the author is really discussing the situation under Antiochus Epiphanes though he is not mentioned by name, only called "a contemptible person" (Daniel 11:21). The whole writing is aimed at encouraging the Jews to be faithful and loyal to their traditions. "The people who know their God shall stand firm and take action" (Daniel 11:32). It is interesting to read this book along with the history of the Maccabean period to see how the writer uses the developments of the time even though he is writing as if they had not yet taken place—and all for the encouragement of those who should never lose their trust in God. In the end, he says, "there shall be a time of trouble, such as never has been since there was a nation till that time; but at that time your people shall be delivered, every one whose name shall be found written in the book" (Daniel 12:1).

22

WHY DO MEN SUFFER?

ALREADY WE HAVE SEEN how the Old Testament contains many kinds of literature. We have read a great deal of history, some fiction, legends, myths, sermons, prophecies, laws.

Like people in all times and places, the Hebrews thought a great deal about deep questions rising out of their life experiences. Some of their writers tried to look at these questions and see what answers they could find through meditation and thinking. The result was several writings that have always held a great deal of interest for readers in every succeeding generation. We shall be studying these in the next three chapters.

First, let us consider the book of Job. Perhaps you may have heard of a play which was running in New York and some other cities during 1959 and 1960 called *J.B.* It was very popular among theatre-goers and won the famous Pulitzer Prize for drama. The author, Archibald MacLeish, drew his inspiration for the play from the biblical book of Job. This is one instance of how the people of every age are exposed in fresh ways to ideas that they cannot really understand without knowing the Bible.

Job is a kind of drama also, though not the kind that was written for the theatre. It is really a long conversation between Job and his friends, with God also taking part in it.

You will notice that the first chapter and part of the last chapter are written in prose, while all the rest of the writing is in poetry. The King James Version (Authorized Version) does not show this clearly, but the Revised Standard Version, as well as other recent versions, does so. We should say one thing here about Hebrew poetry in order to understand it as we read. It is not like our English poetry, which has rhyme and meter (matching sounds and measured syllables). Usually there are two lines, the second of which repeats what is in the first, from a slightly different viewpoint. This is called "parallelism." Here is an example:

> But now, hear my speech, O Job,
>   and listen to all my words.
> Behold, I open my mouth;
>   the tongue in my mouth speaks.
> My words declare the uprightness of my heart,
>   and what my lips know they speak sincerely.
> The spirit of God has made me,
>   and the breath of the Almighty gives me life. . . . (Job
>   33:1–4).

The author seems to have taken an old idea and tried to look at it in a new light. It had long been believed that the righteous would prosper, and that misfortune was punishment for wrong-doing. Yet here was a man who had been very righteous, but he suffered very much. The question, then, is this: Why do righteous people have to suffer? They don't always, of course; but why should they ever have to?

Job is shown as a good man who is praised even in the heavenly council for his faithfulness. One of the members of the council raises doubts about Job. Is he being good only because all had gone prosperously with him? "Does Job fear God for nought?" (Job 1:9). To test him, God sends a series of terrible misfortunes: his cattle and servants are killed by raiders; his sons and daughters are killed in a hurricane. Still Job remains faithful: "Naked I came from my mother's womb, and naked shall I return; the Lord gave, and the Lord has taken away; blessed be the name of the Lord"

(Job 1:21). A still harder test is given him; he is afflicted with some dreadful disease so that he has to sit on the town's refuse heap away from everyone. His friends come to console him but can do nothing for him. In all this suffering, Job does not curse God but remains faithful. Thus far, the prologue. In the epilogue, God answers Job's prayer and restores to him health and even greater prosperity than he had known before.

In between the prologue and the epilogue (the two prose sections), there are the great poems. It is thought that the poetry was inserted by its writer in the framework of the old story about the righteous man Job. The poems, you will note, are conversations between Job and his friends who come to try to cheer him up, as it were; at least they want to try to help him understand his problem. There are three sets of conversation which are really speeches by the friends Eliphaz, Bildad, and Zophar, and Job's replies to them.

In the prologue and epilogue Job is shown as a very patient man who does not complain about his troubles. In the poem, however, he complains a great deal. He curses the day of his birth: "Let that day be darkness!" (Job 3:4); "I am not at ease, nor am I quiet; I have no rest; but trouble comes" (Job 3:26). He protests to God about all that has befallen him: "For he crushes me with a tempest, and multiplies my wounds without cause; he will not let me get my breath, but fills me with bitterness" (Job 9:17–18). He feels locked away from God and cries: "Oh, that I knew where I might find him, that I might come even to his seat!" (Job 23:3).

Finally God answers Job out of a whirlwind. He tells Job that it is not possible to judge God by man's way of looking at things. Job has been too proud; he has had to be humbled. Job understands in the end:

> Therefore I have uttered what I did not understand,
>   things too wonderful for me, which I did not know. . . .

I had heard of thee by the hearing of the ear,
    but now my eye sees thee;
therefore I despise myself,
    and repent in dust and ashes (Job 42:3, 5–6).

Job does not give an answer to the question, "Why do good people suffer?" The book, nevertheless, does show us how all things fall into place if we first of all recognize God and give Him the glory.

23

WORDS OF WISDOM

THE HEBREWS, unlike the Greeks, were not especially interested in abstract thinking. They were always more interested in actual situations, for they thought of God as controlling all the affairs of men in terms of history. There always were some among the Hebrews who had pondered on the meaning of life and expressed their ideas in wise sayings or poems.

King Solomon had always been regarded in the traditions of the Jews as the wisest of men of old times. It was natural that when books of wisdom literature were put together, he would be cited as the author. In the Old Testament a series of writings is ascribed to Solomon—all three of the books we shall discuss in this chapter, in fact, as well as two of the Psalms (72 and 127) and several of the Apocrypha (books that were not made a part of the official canon of the Hebrew Bible), such as the so-called Wisdom of Solomon and the Odes of Solomon. I Kings 4:32 says that Solomon "uttered three thousand proverbs; and his songs were a thousand and five. . . ." So famous was he that "men came from all peoples to hear the wisdom of Solomon, and from all the kings of the earth, who had heard of his wisdom" (I Kings 4:34).

There is reason to believe that the interest in wisdom literature really did begin in Israel during Solomon's reign, and some of the material in these books may well go back for many generations to his time. Actually, however, most of the material in these books was written in the period after the fall of the nation and later collected into the present books.

Proverbs

Everybody likes a wise saying, a pithy statement that puts a deep truth or observation into only a few words that are easily remembered. We have some modern ones and some that date back to people like Benjamin Franklin. In the book of Proverbs we have literally hundreds of these proverbs, most of which few people know because they have not taken the time to read the book. It is well worth reading, and it will surprise us to discover so many interesting gems.

Many of the proverbs have to do with daily life situations. Some are slightly humorous, like 11:22:

> Like a gold ring in a swine's snout
>   is a beautiful woman without discretion.

Many stretch our minds, like 6:16-19:

> There are six things which the Lord hates,
>   seven are an abomination to him:
> haughty eyes, a lying tongue,
>   and hands that shed innocent blood,
> a heart that devises wicked plans,
>   feet that make haste to run to evil,
> a false witness who breathes out lies,
>   and a man who sows discord among brothers.

Some of them try to explain what wisdom itself is and do so vividly in words we can well remember:

> The fear of the Lord is the beginning of wisdom,
>   and the knowledge of the Holy One is insight (Proverbs
>   9:10).

Ecclesiastes

The book called Ecclesiastes is set forth as "the words of the Preacher." It starts out on a note of what we might call pessimism, as if this is the worst possible of worlds:

I have seen everything that is done under the sun; and behold, all is vanity and a striving after wind" (Ecclesiastes
1:14).

He makes a list of many things which he has experienced
and, looking at them, feels that most of what people do is
empty of meaning.

Really, though, he is not a pessimist, for what he is saying
is that God's purposes are never completely known to men.
"However much man may toil in seeking, he will not find it
[the work of God] out; even though a wise man claims to
know, he cannot find it out" (Ecclesiastes 8:17). He concludes
on a positive note: "Fear God, and keep his commandments;
for this is the whole duty of man. For God will bring every
deed into judgment, with every secret thing, whether good
or evil" (Ecclesiastes 12:13–14).

The Song of Solomon

This writing consists of magnificent love poetry from the
Hebrew. Anyone who likes poetry will like the book for its
poetry alone, apart from its meaning. It has been said that
every young couple who fall in love should read this book
together. St Augustine once made a list of books of the Bible
to use with children, and he put this way down at the bottom
of the list to use only with those who are sufficiently advanced
in years, lest they learn about love of men and women too
soon!

Theologians used to justify the inclusion of this love poetry
in the Bible on the ground that what it really is saying is
that God loves Israel. Christians later used allegory (symbolical speech standing for some hidden meaning) to explain
it as meaning Christ's love for the Church. It also can be
looked at as glorifying one important part of human life,
human love being itself a gift of God to His creatures. The
Hebrews thought of God as sanctifying the whole of life.

24

HYMNS OF PRAISE AND PRAYER

No BOOK OF THE BIBLE has been more consistently and reg-
ularly used in the Christian Church than the book of Psalms.
The reason is that the Psalms were taken over from Jewish
worship of the first century A.D. into the worship of the
early Christians and have continued to be used by the
Christians—as by the Jews—ever since.

The Psalter or Psalms of David is contained in its complete
form in the Book of Common Prayer, pp. 345–525. Psalms
are appointed to be read or sung during Daily Morning and
Evening Prayer. A list, according to the days of the Church
Year, is contained in "Psalms and Lessons for the Christian
Year" and "Psalms and Lessons for Special Occasions" on
pp. x through xliii. "Psalms and Lessons for the Fixed Holy
Days" are on pp. xliv and xlv. Selections of Psalms according
to themes are printed on p. ix, covering such areas as God
the Creator, God's Mercy, Trust in God, In Time of Trouble,
Peace, Preparation for Holy Communion, Thanksgiving after
Holy Communion, and so on. The *Venite, exultemus Dom-
ino,* sung or said during Morning Prayer, is based on lines
from Psalms 95 and 96, and is one of the best-known canticles
of the Church.

In addition to being used constantly in our worship, the
Psalms have been deeply loved by generations of people who
in their private devotions turn to them as familiar helps from
Scripture. Some, like Psalm 23 and Psalm 100, are usually

memorized by Church School children early in their experience at church.

Note that the translation we use in the Book of Common Prayer is not the same as that in the King James Version or the more recent versions. It is a still earlier translation completed in the sixteenth century and has been in continuous use in the Anglican Churches.

The Hymnbook of the Second Temple

The Psalms were used in the worship of the Temple at Jerusalem after its rebuilding. It is thrilling to realize that when we today join in singing the Psalms or reading them responsively, we are sharing in the words of worship used by God's people from ancient times. Here are gathered together a wide variety of themes that have to do with religious living. History is contained in many of them, and in others there is pure devotion of the loftiest sort.

We cannot be sure about the dates in which the various Psalms were composed. Some of them date back to the days before the Exile, but in its present form the collection goes back to the days of the second Temple, so that it is right to call the Psalms "the hymnbook of the second Temple." The use of these Psalms in the Jewish worship can be captured in our imagination by reading Psalms 145 through 150, headed at Psalm 145, "A Song of Praise. Of David," as though they were one continuous song. "Praise the Lord" is the refrain that is repeated again and again. Picture the magnificent procession as it takes place, the voices of the people joining in Psalm 150:

> Praise the Lord!
> Praise God in his sanctuary;
>   praise him in his mighty firmament!
> Praise him for his mighty deeds;
>   praise him according to his exceeding greatness!

Praise him with the trumpet sound;
  praise him with lute and harp!
Praise him with timbrel and dance;
  praise him with strings and pipe!
Praise him with sounding cymbals;
  praise him with loud clashing cymbals!
Let everything that breathes praise the Lord!
Praise the Lord!

Read one of the long historical Psalms like the 78th. There, in capsule form, you have a summary of the long history of Israel, all brought together for the people's present remembering. Note the remembrance of the Exodus and the movement into Canaan:

He smote all the first-born in Egypt,
  the first issue of their strength in the tents of Ham.
Then he led forth his people like sheep,
  and guided them in the wilderness like a flock.
He led them in safety, so that they were not afraid;
  but the sea overwhelmed their enemies.
And he brought them to his holy land,
  to the mountain which his right hand had won.
He drove out nations before them;
  he apportioned them for a possession
  and settled the tribes of Israel in their tents (Psalm 78:51–55).

Apparently musicians played an important part in the Temple worship. In the titles of the Psalms names of leaders of musical guilds are mentioned, persons like Asaph, Ethan, Heman. Many of the Psalms are attributed to David. Whether he actually was responsible for writing any of them, we do not know for sure, but tradition gives many of the Psalms to him. Solomon, too, is mentioned as an author (see, for example, Psalm 127). The so-called "Songs of Ascents," from 120 through 134, were probably used as the people went to

Jerusalem in pilgrimages to the Temple. A good example of these is Psalm 134:

> Come, bless the Lord, all you servants of the Lord,
>   who stand by night in the house of the Lord!
> Lift up your hands to the holy place,
>   and bless the Lord!
> May the Lord bless you from Zion,
>   he who made heaven and earth!

25

PREPARING THE WAY OF THE LORD

THE OLD TESTAMENT's last book to be written was Daniel. There were other writings, called the Apocrypha, which circulated widely and were in the line of development of the Jewish Scriptures. The tradition, however, had developed that prophecy had begun with Moses and ended with the time of Alexander the Great (some said with Ezra). When the rabbis met at Jamnia around A.D. 90 to decide on what books should be included in the canon (authorized Scriptures), they omitted the Apocrypha.

Some parts of the Christian Church, including Anglicanism, have continued to regard the Apocrypha as important "for example of life and instruction of manners; but yet doth it not apply them to establish any doctrine." (See Article VI, "The Articles of Religion," the Book of Common Prayer, p. 604.) Among the more important of these writings are Ecclesiasticus (called also Jesus the Son of Sirach), The Book of Wisdom, The Song of the Three Children, I and II Maccabees. Lessons for Morning and Evening Prayer are occasionally taken from the Apocrypha.

Judaism Continues

Although Scripture was completed, as far as the Old Testament was concerned, by the time of the Maccabees, life went on. Judaism was not by any means ended as a great religion; indeed, even today, it continues as a very important religion in the world scene. Even Israel has re-entered the ranks of the nations in our own century after the many hundreds of years during which the Jews could claim no political homeland. In modern Israel, Judaism is the state religion once again.

To go back to the Maccabees, you will recall we said that by 165 B.C. a Jewish nation was once more in existence on Palestinian soil under the rulership of the Maccabee family, who were called the Hasmoneans. Theirs was a short-lived kingdom because in 64 B.C. Syria and Palestine were taken over as a part of the rising Roman Empire.

Several religious parties rose within Judaism. They are important to identify because they were active in Palestine during the life of our Lord.

The Sadducees were one of these parties. Most of them were aristocrats, members of families that held high position among the priests and political leaders. They were very conservative, looking to the past rather than the future. They were convinced that sacrifice and worship should be conducted in strict accordance with the Law of Moses. Politically they were willing to co-operate with foreign powers as long as nothing interfered too much with the worship of the Temple.

The Pharisees were a stricter group even than the Sadducees, but in a different way. They looked to the future when God would act to restore Israel to His chosen people. They did not believe that Jews should have relation with Gentiles, and they insisted on a careful carrying out of all the Mosaic Law, such as rules about diet, fasting, and so on. On numerous occasions Jesus came into conflict with the Pharisees, who thought Him unfaithful to the religion of their fathers.

Still another group were the Essenes. We have heard a lot about the people in recent years since the discovery of the Dead Sea Scrolls at Qumran. They were something like a

monastic community. They withdrew from the world to practice their devotion to the Torah, and they believed that God
would come suddenly to restore His Kingdom.

The Zealots were another group. They were militant for
Judaism and felt that the only thing to do was to fight the
battles of the Lord against all foreign powers. In this they
were like the original Maccabean revolutionists. It is thought
that perhaps Judas Iscariot, the disciple who betrayed Jesus,
belonged to the Zealot group.

The Roman Rule

When Palestine came under Roman rule, the Jews were
permitted a considerable measure of freedom in carrying
on their religious practices. They even had their own king,
although he was subject to Roman governors. In the time
of Jesus Christ this was the situation. The king of the Jews
at the time of Jesus' birth was Herod the Great.

The Roman policy of permitting subject peoples to have
freedom within limits was part of the deliberate Roman
policy to maintain peace in the world. This was the famous
Pax Romana, the Roman peace. Rome was interested in
building up her civilization wherever her power held sway,
and as long as her colonial subjects did not show signs of
revolt, she left them pretty much to themselves. The Jews
had had an especially strong record of revolt under the
Maccabees, and they were considered always to be a "touchy"
point within the Empire: thus their worship continued without too much Roman control.

There had been taking place, meanwhile, a movement
called the Diaspora, the scattering of Jews to various parts
of Europe and Asia. It has been said that there were more
Jews outside Palestine than in it at the beginning of New
Testament times. This meant that Jewish synagogues were
to be found in widely scattered cities. When St. Paul began

his missionary journeys, these synagogues and communities of Jews were points of contact for the spread of the Christian Gospel. We should mention also the excellent communication methods that existed at this period, in comparison with earlier times, and the roads and shipping routes. All of these helped to prepare the way for the rapid growth of Christianity which was soon to begin.

Part IV
THE NEW TESTAMENT

26

PROCLAIMING THE GOOD NEWS

THE TITLE PAGE of the latter part of the Bible often contains the following: "The New Covenant, Commonly Called the New Testament of Our Lord and Saviour Jesus Christ."

The early Christians could not think of themselves except against the background of the acts of God by which He had brought into being the community dedicated to His will and purpose: Israel. Yet they were conscious of being brought into a new community at the same time, one which God had called together by His new act in sending Jesus Christ to be the world's Saviour.

This is the theme of the whole body of writings which grew up in the new community of the Christian Church. The opening words of the Letter to the Hebrews states it this way:

> In many and various ways God spoke of old to our fathers by the prophets; but in these last days he has spoken to us by a Son, whom he appointed the heir of all things, through whom also he created the world (Hebrews 1:1–2).

It was their conviction that God had acted in a new way not in order to upset all that He had done in the long past through the people of Israel, but in order to complete the redemption of the world. Jesus Christ was indeed a new act of God, by whom mankind was given a new life and a new salvation. All of this was seen against the background of the old.

First It Was Lived

For many years before any Christian wrote down a single word about our Lord and what He meant to the world, the followers of Christ were living together in the new fellowship of the Church. They had first heard the Gospel (which means "the good news") from the lips and acts of Jesus while He was on earth, preaching, teaching, healing, and ministering. After the Crucifixion and Resurrection, He was no longer with them in the flesh, but they knew that His Risen Being was with them still, guiding and sustaining them.

Now it was they, who He had said would be His body, who were to go into the world proclaiming the mighty acts by which God had brought His loving redemption to all people. This they were best able to do by word of mouth and by deeds of loving service, both to one another in the Church and to those not yet baptized for whom also Christ had lived and died and risen again. Christ had told them that they were to "Go . . . and make disciples of all nations, baptizing them in the name of the Father and of the Son and of the Holy Spirit, teaching them to observe all that I have commanded you; and lo, I am with you always, to the close of the age" (Matthew 28:19–20). That was a terribly important commission, especially when the disciples realized how few and weak they were. Few of them were people of importance as far as the world was concerned. The original Apostles and the other disciples were simple folk. Now they had this exciting new task to perform, to tell the good news to all who would hear.

For a long time they were too busy going about their own communities winning converts to think of writing anything down permanently, but they did remember vividly the sayings of Jesus. The traveling preachers would repeat the parables (stories) He had used. Whenever they gathered together for the Supper of the Lord which He had commanded them to keep, they would be reminded of His words to the Apostles at the Last Supper in the upper room at Jerusalem. They knew by heart the sayings that had meant most to them, such as the Beatitudes. They would frequently repeat the prayer He had taught them, "Our Father, who art in heaven." It must be remembered, too, they were all Jews who, like their Lord, had been nurtured in the faith of Israel and shared the same traditions and Scriptures.

Thus there developed an "oral tradition." We in the modern world have available so many printed materials, not to mention other forms of information and communication like radio and television, that we can scarcely understand how Oriental people of the ancient times depended so much on memory. If we want to look up something, all we need to do is go to a library or to a book on our own shelves. Books were non-existent in the sense we have them. Scrolls were few and far between. Furthermore, only a few of the people could read. It is not at all surprising, therefore, that the oral tradition proved to be very dependable when finally the records of the life of Jesus and the Early Church were put into writing.

The Greek Language

When St. Paul began to write letters, and the evangelists put together the records about Jesus in the four gospels, they wrote in the Greek language. The spoken language of the people in Palestine was Aramaic (a Semitic language similar to Hebrew). Why, then, were the New Testament writings put into Greek? You will recall that Alexander the Great had spread Hellenism (Greek civilization) throughout the broad empire he controlled. One result was that Greek came to be spoken almost everywhere. By the first century A.D., this was the almost universal language in which people would communicate when they set things down in writing. The Greek of the New Testament is not the same as classical Greek (like that the philosopher Plato used), but the spoken Greek. A comparison might be the difference between the kind of English a great scholar would use in a book and the simpler English we use as we talk with one another day by day.

As far as we know, Jesus Himself did not write anything. Certainly, if He did, nothing has survived. The earliest writings of the New Testament were St. Paul's letters. His writings are important to us because they give us a picture of the kind of preaching and teaching the first Christians heard. The largest number of the New Testament writings, as we shall see, come from St. Paul.

The four gospels were written much later, after St. Paul had been dead for some years. The word *gospel* with a small "g" refers to the type of writing the evangelists put together. With the passing of the years, various people had started to write down notes of various kinds about Jesus—facts concerning His life, sayings He had uttered, stories He had told, and so on, in order that these might be preserved or used by Christians in their work of spreading the good news. The compilers of the gospels used these notes plus recollections of the Apostles. They were not trying to write full biographies of Jesus in the way modern writers have written up the lives of famous people like Abraham Lincoln and hundreds of others. As we shall see, they were chiefly interested to tell others what God had done through His Son.

As we study the books of the New Testament, we shall see that above all they are writings that grew out of the life of the Christian Church. These writers were not just individuals writing for a public. They were giving expression to their religious faith, just as the writers of the Old Testament books in their day had been writing out of the common experiences of Israel.

27

THE GOSPEL OF THE SON OF GOD

NOTE THE TITLES of the four gospels in the New Testament. They are all listed as "the gospel according to" followed by the names associated with the books, Sts. Matthew, Mark, Luke, and John. "According to" is not used in quite the same way as "by." It implies a certain amount of interpretation by the writer. These writers were not producing completely individual work. They were putting together material from the oral tradition and whatever written notes were available, arranging the material, adding other material which only they had at hand, until the finished writings were ready.

The way a writer begins his work is always important. When we look at the first sentences of each of these gospels, we get a clue as to the framework, and the purpose of the compiler.

First we shall consider the gospel according to St. Mark. Why do we start with his work instead of St. Matthew's which stands as the first book in the New Testament? The reason is that we know from the work of scholars that St. Mark was the first of the four evangelists to write.

The Earliest Gospel

One reason for our knowing that this is the first gospel to have been written is the fact that the authors of the gospels according to St. Matthew and St. Luke used a great deal of material taken directly from Mark. They would have had to have St. Mark's gospel in their hands when they did their writing. These three gospels are sometimes called the "Synoptic Gospels." If you look up the word "synoptic" in a dictionary, you will find that it comes from Greek roots meaning "looking together." It is possible to see these three gospels as they are related to one another in what is called a "harmony of the gospels." If you set Matthew, Mark, and Luke side by side in parallel passages, you will find that much of Mark is contained in the other two. Perhaps your teacher or rector will be able to supply you with a harmony so that you can see this for yourself. A good place to see this relationship of materials is to compare Matthew 21:23–27, Mark 11:27–33, and Luke 20:1–8. It is interesting, also, that St. Matthew and St. Luke had some things in common which are not found at all in Mark. Compare, for example, Matthew 8:19–22 and Luke 9:57–60. St. John's gospel stands by itself, as we shall see, although he, too, seems to have been quite familiar with Mark.

Why It Was Written

Several facts led to the writing of the gospels. St. Mark (whose name, according to Acts 12:12, was John Mark) was closely involved in the missionary spread of Christianity. A relative of St. Barnabas', he went with that missionary and St. Paul on their first missionary journey (Acts 13:5). From I Peter 5:13 we learn that he was later in Rome with St. Peter. From these chief leaders in the Church he doubtless learned a great deal of information about the details of Jesus' life and ministry. From hearing their preaching and teaching he had every chance to know who the Lord was and how He was thought of by the Church.

Mark was a "natural" for writing down these accounts. It was important for someone to do that for several reasons. First, the Christians were being persecuted under the Emperor Nero, who in A.D. 64–65 blamed the Christians for having started a fire that destroyed more than half of the city of Rome. They were completely innocent, of course, but this gave the Emperor an "out" for blaming someone for the fire and also for getting rid of many of the leaders of the growing religion, which he did not like because it did not recognize the Emperor as divine.

Also, the people who had been eyewitnesses of Jesus' ministry were rapidly dying off because of age, if not from persecution, and it was important that something be written down before all was forgotten. Those who were being persecuted, too, would get strength and help from being able to read of our Lord's sufferings and death and Resurrection, knowing that they were being called to be strong through Him.

If the gospel of Mark was written about the year A.D. 65, probably St. Mark was living at that time in Rome. He writes in a clear way that would have appealed to those who would read the book—converts to Judaism from the Greek world, slaves who had been educated (they were often teachers), and citizens of the Roman government who spoke the Greek that was used widely throughout the empire.

The Story Is Told

Notice how the gospel begins: "The beginning of the gospel of Jesus Christ, the Son of God." In 1:1 St. Mark announces right away who this person is of whom he is writing. He is not going to try to prove to the reader that Jesus is the Son of God. He is absolutely honest at the very outset in telling the reader that this is the Saviour of the world, God's only Son, about whom he is going to write. Jesus is shown to be the fulfillment of Israel's ancient hope for a Messiah.

After John the Baptist's preaching on the need for repenting of sin, Jesus appears on the scene. His Baptism in the

Jordan River marks the beginning of His public ministry, for soon after His forty days' meditation and prayer in the wilderness He comes into Galilee, "preaching the gospel of God, and saying, 'The time is fulfilled, and the kingdom of God is at hand; repent, and believe in the gospel'" (Mark 1:14–15).

Chapters 1:14 to 8:26 give details of Jesus' ministry. He preaches often, heals many, and wins a popular response from large numbers of people. The religious leaders start to become suspicious of Him, however, and He is considered to be a dangerous threat to the traditional Jewish faith. By the time He comes to His home region around Nazareth, the leaders of the synagogue reject Him (Mark 6:1–6).

Meanwhile He has gathered around Him twelve intimate followers. The number twelve is significant. Remember the Twelve Tribes of Israel. Jesus may have intended, by appointing that number of Apostles, to stress the fact that He was gathering together the "New Israel of God." That is one of the ways in which the interpreters of the faith, like St. Paul, thought of the Church.

In Chapter 8:27–33 we come to a very important point in the gospel. This is the conversation Jesus had with His Apostles as they traveled through Caesarea Philippi. They pause to take account of His ministry to date. He asks them, "Who do men say that I am?" The answer comes that the people think of Him as being a prophet like John the Baptist, Elijah, or some other. He presses the question to them: "But who do *you* say that I am?" Jesus wants to know if His own most intimate friends are beginning to understand the nature of His work in the world. St. Peter immediately replies, "You are the Christ."

Apparently Jesus did not want them to spread this word around too freely. He must have known that if the claim that He was the Messiah (*Christ* is the Greek word for *Messiah* and means *Anointed One*) got around, He would be silenced by the authorities before He had completed His mission. Also, if He thought of Himself as Messiah, it was not in the popular sense of expecting a powerful deliverer who would set up an earthly kingdom. He was to be like the Messiah talked of by the Second Isaiah, upon whom the sins of the world would be laid. (See Isaiah 53. Think of the ancient Christian hymn which we use sometimes during the Holy Communion, the *Agnus Dei,* "Lamb of God, that takest away the sins of the world. . . .")

At any rate, from this time on Jesus began to instruct the Apostles "that the Son of man must suffer many things, and be rejected by the elders and the chief priests and the scribes, and be killed, and after three days rise again" (Mark 8:31).

The rest of St. Mark's gospel points toward the events that were to happen at Jerusalem during the last week of Jesus' life—His approaching Passion and death and Resurrection. The importance of these final events is indicated by the fact that the largest part of the gospels deals with those happenings that we recall each year during Holy Week. In the memory of the first Christian eyewitnesses, those were the mighty acts of God for man's salvation. More detail was remembered concerning those last days than all the rest of Jesus' thirty-three or so years on earth.

You will note that in the Revised Standard Version the gospel of Mark ends with Chapter 16:8. Some additional verses contained in earlier versions, like the King James, are put in a footnote. The earliest manuscripts end with verse 8. It is possible that the last page of St. Mark's manuscript was accidentally torn off, or that he was interrupted before he could finish. In any event, the verses from 9 through 20 were added much later in order to finish the book.

The earliest gospel is the shortest of the four. It "marches." The story of our Lord is set forth vividly and powerfully.

As we read it, we remember that here we have the facts of the gospel from sources as close to the Apostles as they could possibly be. We see how Jesus appeared to them as He appears to us still, the Son of God.

28

THE SON OF DAVID

St. Matthew's gospel comes first in the New Testament canon. Since this gospel interprets Jesus in the fullest and deepest sense as the fulfiller of the Old Testament prophecies and hopes, it was natural that it should have been placed first. It has sometimes been called "the bridge between the Testaments" for that reason.

It starts: "The book of the genealogy of Jesus Christ, the son of David, the son of Abraham" (Matthew 1:1). This leaves no doubt as to the writer's intention. He wants to show that God in the fullness of time has acted to complete the work He started with the very first Patriarch, old Abraham, "the father of the people Israel."

Throughout the gospel, Jesus' messianic purpose is stressed. At the time of His birth Gentile (non-Jewish) wise men come to pay their respects to Him in His cradle. He is born in Bethlehem in fulfillment of the prophecy in Micah 5:2.

> And you, O Bethlehem, in the land of Judah,
> are by no means least among the rulers of Judah;
> for from you shall come a ruler
> who will govern my people Israel (Matthew 2:6).

The Baptism of Jesus is set forth as His anointing by the Spirit to be God's "beloved Son, with whom I am well pleased" (Matthew 3:13–17). After the Temptation, Jesus goes forth to preach and teach and heal, "that what was spoken by the prophet Isaiah might be fulfilled," bringing light to the people "who sat in darkness" (Matthew 4:12–17). Jesus is referred to eight times in this gospel as "the Son of David."

Other Characteristics of the Gospel

This gospel contains several big chunks of material which are usually referred to as "discourses" of Jesus. These are collections of sayings that evidently were treasured in the Early Church and gathered together into their present form in order that they could be preserved. Also, it is thought that maybe the writer had in mind making available these sayings in order that they could be used for teaching purposes as they are very conveniently arranged into groups.

We should note that the famous Sermon on the Mount is one of these groups of discourses. As the gospel arranges the Sermon on the Mount, we get the impression that Jesus spoke all these words in a connected address on one occasion. It is more likely that the writer gathered various related sayings and put them together in their present form, for no one was present to make a recording of Jesus' words exactly as He had spoken them. They are some of the greatest teachings of our Lord. Christians will always turn to Chapters 5 through 7 for the undying words of Christ. Here are such familiar words as the Beatitudes (5:1–11) and the Lord's Prayer (6:9–13). In connection with the Lord's Prayer, note that the prayer taught by our Lord ends with "But deliver us from evil." This is the form in which we use it in the Litany and in certain other worship forms such as a Penitential Office for Ash Wednesday (see the Book of Common Prayer, p. 58, p. 61). Usually, however, we end the Lord's Prayer with the ascription, "For thine is the kingdom, and the power, and the glory, for ever and ever," as in the Holy Communion (Prayer Book, p. 82). This is considered to be a later addition coming out of the Early Church's worship.

The Revised Standard Version prints it in a footnote, stating that "other authorities, some ancient, add, in some form, 'For thine is the kingdom and the power and the glory, for ever. Amen.' " (Note how St. Luke's gospel uses a part of the material in the Lord's Prayer. See Luke 11:2–4.)

Other sections of sayings of Jesus include the charge to the Apostles, to whom He gave "authority over unclean spirits, to cast them out, and to heal every disease and every infirmity" in Chapter 10; a series of parables about the Kingdom of God in Chapter 13; teachings concerning humility and forgiveness in Chapter 18; and Chapters 24 and 25, which deal with the end of the age.

Note that all these discourses refer in some way to the Kingdom of God. Jesus taught that the Kingdom toward which the prophets pointed had now dawned, and those who came to God in faith could already enter the blessings of the Kingdom. Those who did respond became members of the New Israel, the Church, against which the powers of death could not prevail. (See Matthew 16:18.) God calls men into His Kingdom, and man's first responsibility should be to seek "his kingdom and his righteousness" (Matthew 6:33).

Who Wrote the Gospel?

St. Matthew, one of the twelve Apostles, was regarded in the tradition of the Early Church as the author of the first gospel in the canon. (See Matthew 9:9 for a description of St. Matthew's call to be an Apostle.) The gospel itself does not mention who the author is, and we have no outside information that is positive. A bishop of the early second century, named Papias, wrote a statement to the effect that "Matthew compiled the oracles in the Hebrew language." Matthew was probably the compiler of the sayings of Jesus which were then taken over for re-writing into the larger gospel by some other person whose name we do not know.

The "oracles" Papias referred to probably meant St. Matthew's collection of the sayings. One thing we can be quite sure of, the compiler of this gospel was a Jewish Christian writing for Jews, for he interprets our Lord clearly as "the Son of David."

It is thought that this gospel was written between A.D. 60 and 85, more likely nearer the latter date. At least it was composed after Mark had been written—that we know—and probably after the destruction of the Temple in A.D. 70 by the Romans.

29

LORD OF ALL

THE THIRD GOSPEL, St. Luke, was called by Renan, a famous biblical scholar of the nineteenth century, "the most beautiful book in the world." Generations of Christians have turned to this gospel not only for the religious message it contains but because of its lovely language. The author was certainly not trying to write a book for artistic enjoyment first of all, for he, like the other evangelists, had a serious Christian purpose in mind. The fact is, nevertheless, that his writing contains spiritual gems that put us forever in his debt.

Here, for example, are the wonderful stories of the Annunciation and the Nativity of our Lord. Mary, the Virgin who learns that she is to give birth to the Child who "will be called holy, the Son of God," utters the words that have become a part of the daily worship of the whole catholic Church:

> My soul magnifies the Lord,
> and my spirit rejoices in God my Savior,
> for he has regarded the low estate of his handmaiden.
> For behold, henceforth all generations will call me blessed;
> for he who is mighty has done great things for me,
> and holy is his name (Luke 1:46–49).

See p. 26 of the Book of Common Prayer for the version used in Daily Evening Prayer. The *Nunc Dimittis* (p. 28 of the Prayer Book) is another of these gems taken over into the Church's liturgical life. It comes from St. Luke 2:29–32, the

words of the old man Simeon who rejoices over the fulfillment
of his longing for the coming of the Messiah. In St. Luke
1:68–79, we read the words of rejoicing by Zechariah over the
birth of his son, John the Baptist. This is used in our order
for Morning Prayer on p. 14 of the Prayer Book as the *Bene-
dictus*. These passages were probably used in the Church's
worship before the gospel writer incorporated them in his
book. Being preserved in his writing, they have become the
cherished inheritance of the whole Christian Church.

A Two-Part Document

Luke is really Part I of a two-part writing, sometimes referred to as Luke-Acts, for the same man wrote both these
present books in our New Testament.

You can see the connection by comparing the opening
verses of Luke and Acts. In St. Luke 1:1–4 it is said:

> Inasmuch as many have undertaken to compile a narrative
> of the things which have been accomplished among us, just
> as they were delivered to us by those who from the beginning
> were eyewitnesses and ministers of the word, it seemed good
> to me also, having followed all things closely for some time
> past, to write an orderly account for you, most excellent
> Theophilus, that you may know the truth concerning the
> things of which you have been informed.

Note how the author does not say that he is going to com-
pile merely an account of the Gospel of Jesus Christ in terms
of our Lord's life taken by itself. He wants to discuss in an
orderly way all the things that have happened—and that
would go on beyond the earthly life and Resurrection of
Jesus Christ into the life of the Early Christian community
as it had developed to date.

Then, in Acts 1:1 we read:

> In the first book, O Theophilus, I have dealt with all that
> Jesus began to do and teach, until the day when he was

taken up, after he had given commandment through the Holy Spirit to the apostles whom he had chosen.

Then he proceeds to continue the narrative, beginning with the resurrected Jesus' promise that the Holy Spirit would come upon them and they would be His witnesses "to the end of the earth," going on to the Ascension and Pentecost.

Both prefaces are addressed to Theophilus. Was there a man by that name or does it mean, as in the Greek language, some "lover of God"? The fact that the same person is addressed in both ties the two together.

Who Was Luke?

We do not know a great deal about St. Luke, except for three references in the New Testament. In Colossians 4:14 he is referred to as "the beloved physician." We read of him as a close acquaintance of St. Paul's in Philemon 24 and in II Timothy 4:11. In addition to these actual references, there are traditions in the Church that he was born in Antioch in Syria.

We know from material in Luke that the writer was interested in medical subjects or at least showed some familiarity with them. Also, from passages in Acts, as in Chapter 16:10–17, where suddenly "we" is introduced instead of the third person "he" or "they," it seems that he was a companion of St. Paul's on the missionary trek. For reasons like these most scholars assume that it was indeed St. Luke who wrote the two-part document that we have in our New Testament as two separate books, the gospel according to St. Luke and the Acts of the Apostles.

The Sections of the Gospel

Like Matthew, Luke used a large portion of material from Mark. The gospel according to Luke also has some material in common with Matthew which Mark does not contain. In addition, there are many things that only St. Luke recorded, especially referring to the beginnings of Jesus' life and the journey from Galilee to the capital city, Jerusalem.

The sections of Luke can be outlined something as follows:

1. Chapters 1:5 through 2. Jesus' birth and boyhood. (Note that the only incident we have from His early youth is His visit with Joseph and Mary to the Temple at Jerusalem when He was twelve years of age.)

2. Chapters 3 through 4:14. John the Baptist, Jesus' Baptism, the Temptation.

3. Chapters 4:14 through 9:50. The Galilean ministry.

4. Chapters 9:51 through 19:44. Going toward Jerusalem.

5. Chapters 19:45 through 24. The last events: Crucifixion, Resurrection.

Scholars think that Luke was written about A.D. 75.

Of the characteristics of Luke we can mention two especially important ones. First, St. Luke is eager to show that Jesus came to those who were weak, downtrodden, and in need. This is stressed even at the beginning of the gospel when Mary refers to herself as being of "low estate." Jesus begins His ministry by reading in the synagogue from the book of Isaiah:

The Spirit of the Lord is upon me,
because he has anointed me to preach good news to the poor
    (Luke 4:18).

Sympathy and compassion are qualities of our Lord's which He urged upon His hearers. Secondly, Jesus Christ is interpreted as being the Saviour of the world, all people, and not exclusively the Messiah who had been expected by the Jews. Like the other evangelists, St. Luke makes it clear that Jesus grows up and works in the tradition of Israel, but God's work through Him is not limited to Israel. He is the Christ for the world.

30

THE WORD BECAME FLESH

WHEN WE LOOK AT the fourth gospel, the one according to John, we no longer are dealing with the "Synoptic Gospels." To be sure, this book is dealing with the selfsame Lord and the same Gospel of Jesus Christ, but there is no longer the same literary inter-relationship with the other gospels, such as we saw existed among Mark, Matthew, and Luke.

Furthermore, the writer has a different point of view from which he looks at Jesus. He wants the reader to know that Jesus is the fulfillment of Jewish expectations, as Matthew also desired to do. He wants the reader to see that He who has redeemed mankind is identical with the very Word of God, who existed at the beginning of time and has now come to earth in fleshly form in a real Person, Jesus.

The prologue of the fourth gospel, the first eighteen verses of chapter 1, says the bold fact—"the Word became flesh and dwelt among us, full of grace and truth; we have beheld his glory, glory as of the only Son from the Father" (John 1:14).

Does that remind you of anything you say frequently in church? Think of the Nicene Creed which we use at the Holy Eucharist. "Begotten, not made; Being of one substance with the Father; By whom all things were made: Who for us men and for our salvation came down from heaven, and was incarnate by the Holy Ghost of the Virgin Mary, And was made man. . . ." (The Book of Common Prayer, p. 71).

The whole of the gospel of John gives incidents that show Christ in these exalted terms. In the opening six chapters we read dramatic incidents that point out the glory of the Son of God. Then comes evidence of the clash between the authorities and Jesus, how more and more He is being hated and hounded to death, on one hand, while those who are nearest to Him share in ever deeper fellowship with Him. (See, for instance, the relations between Jesus and the family of Martha, Mary, and Lazarus in Chapters 11 and 12 and the anointing of Jesus' feet with precious ointment by Mary, in John 12:1–8.) Then there are Chapters 13–17 in which Jesus takes His Apostles deeply into His confidence and gives them deep, lasting instruction. Among these chapters, 17 is one of the most magnificent in the whole Bible. It is Jesus' farewell prayer, in which He asks of His heavenly Father:

> Father, the hour has come; glorify thy Son that the Son may glorify thee, since thou hast given him power over all flesh, to give eternal life to all whom thou hast given him. And this is eternal life, that they know thee the only true God, and Jesus Christ whom thou hast sent . . . (John 17:1–3).

Then follows, finally, the account of the trial and Crucifixion and the Resurrection.

The last chapter in the book deals with Resurrection appearances of Christ. He gives the command to St. Peter, "Feed my sheep," a command that has been taken seriously by the ministers of Christ across the centuries. This comes to its focus in the celebration of the Eucharist when the priest gives to the worshipping people the very Bread of Life, the Sacrament in which Christ Himself has promised to be present to the end of time.

Which John?

Scholars have debated for many years over who the John was who is called by tradition the author of the fourth gospel. Many insist that it was the Apostle John, "the disciple whom

Jesus loved" (see John 21:20), who wrote the book. Since it evidently was not written, or at least sent around to the churches, until A.D. 90 to 100, the Apostle would have been a very old man indeed at the time he wrote the gospel. There was apparently another John, called the Elder John by Papias, who wrote in the early second century. The latter man lived, perhaps, in Ephesus, a city where this gospel and the letters, I, II, and III John, seem to have originated. Many thus think that John the Elder was the writer. In any event, it was written by an eyewitness or a disciple of an eyewitness.

Do not let this matter of ascribing authorship of books, when it cannot be proved who wrote them, disturb you. It was quite common in the ancient world to associate a book with a well-known person. Sometimes this was done only with the view to honoring the name of a great person. It had nothing to do with dishonesty, as we would certainly regard it today.

Note how the fourth gospel's writer presents Jesus' words. In the other three gospels, Jesus speaks usually in parables or short, pithy sentences; here He speaks in long, rather involved paragraphs. The order of events is differently presented, also. The Temple is cleansed at the beginning rather than at the end of Jesus' ministry. Most of the ministry takes place not in Galilee, but in the south.

We can be especially grateful to this gospel for certain details it gives of the Last Supper of our Lord with His Apostles in Jerusalem, when He washes their feet and tells them: "Truly, truly, I say to you, a servant is not greater than his master; nor is he who is sent greater than he who sent him. If you know these things, blessed are you if you do them" (John 13:16–17). John does not tell of the blessing of the bread and the wine. That account is given in Matthew 26:17–30, Luke 22:7–23, and, as we shall see, in I Corinthians 11:23–26.

31

THE WORK OF THE HOLY SPIRIT

THE SECOND PART of St. Luke's two-part work takes us into the first days of the Christian Church following the Resurrection and Ascension of our Lord. It is fortunate for all of us in succeeding generations that St. Luke wrote this book, for it is actually the only full source of information we have concerning the beginnings of the organized Church. Among other things, this book of the Acts of the Apostles outlines the events out of which grew the various letters of St. Paul which make up the remaining bulk of the New Testament after the four gospels.

We have to use a little imagination to realize what it must have seemed like to the earliest Christians to have their Master taken from them. He had charged them to go into all the world, baptizing and teaching in His name and that of the Father and the Holy Spirit. (See Matthew 28:19-20.) That is sometimes called the Great Commission.

The first things they had to confront were problems in their own little company. They had the joy and rapture of meeting together for the breaking of bread and for prayers (Acts 2:46-47). They found that their fellowship was attracting new recruits who wanted to share in the life of Christ, but they had some practical matters that had to be taken care of promptly. After Judas' betrayal of Jesus and his later suicide, they had to choose someone to take his place among the Apostles. The lot fell upon Matthias.

They had to arrange their economic life. Apparently they

arrived at a manner of life only after some difficulty. It had been agreed that they would have all things in common and to that end it was agreed each would sell his property and bring the proceeds into a common treasury. One couple, Ananias and Sapphira, kept back some money. (We read of what happened to them in Acts 5:1–11.) The method of common sharing was adopted partly because the first Christians expected the end of the age before long when Christ would suddenly return to set up His reign on earth.

The Spirit Comes

All necessary practical problems were taken in their stride in the Early Church. These Christians were first of all filled with the tremendous excitement of belonging to the fellowship of Christ. Because the Holy Spirit had come to dwell in their midst, they no longer felt alone and defeated, but filled with spiritual power. The story of the Pentecost experience, which we commemorate at Whitsuntide each year, is told in Acts 2. What happened was that, as Christ had promised, the Christians became aware of being the Spirit-led community of believers. Now they were to go forth into the world able and empowered to fulfill the commission Christ had given them in His Resurrection.

The inner life of the Church and the Church's witness to the world was to be constantly renewed by the Holy Spirit. This is one of the basic themes of the Acts of the Apostles. The earliest Church was still related to the Jewish community in that all the first Christians were Jews until the Christian missionaries moved out into the Gentile world. What differentiated the Christians from the Jews was their devotion to Jesus Christ, who had brought them into a new covenant with God, and eventually, of course, their worship. At first the Christians continued to attend the synagogues for their worship as had been their practice for many years, but they would also meet with their fellow-Christians for the Sacrament of the Lord's Supper and for special prayers and actions of the community. This led, finally, to a complete separation from the synagogues as far as their worship was concerned. They continued, however, to use some elements of the Jewish worship, such as the Psalms, as we have seen.

Early Christian Preaching

In those times, as ever since, preaching was a principal method for telling others about the faith. In the Acts we find some "samples" of the Apostles' preaching. For example, we read in Acts 3 how St. Peter and St. John healed a man from lameness at the "Beautiful Gate" of the Temple. Every day that lame man had sat there asking passers-by for alms. St. Peter says to him, "I have no silver or gold, but I give you what I have; in the name of Jesus Christ of Nazareth, walk" (Acts 3:6). Immediately the man stands up, enters the Temple with the two Apostles, "leaping and praising God." People gather around in curiosity, for they recognize the man as one who had sat for years at the Temple gate begging. To the people who gathered, St. Peter proceeds to preach the Gospel:

Men of Israel, why do you wonder at this, or why do you stare at us, as though by our own power or piety we had made him walk? The God of Abraham and of Isaac and of Jacob, the God of our fathers, glorified his servant Jesus, whom you delivered up and denied in the presence of Pilate, when he had decided to release him. But you denied the Holy and Righteous One, and asked for a murderer to be granted to you, and killed the Author of life, whom God raised from the dead. To this we are witnesses. And his name, by faith in his name, has made this man strong whom you see and know; and the faith which is through Jesus has given the man this perfect health in the presence of you all (Acts 3:12–16).

St. Peter clinches his sermon by confronting the listeners with a need for a decision about Christ. "Repent therefore, and turn again, that your sins may be blotted out, that times of refreshing may come from the presence of the Lord, and that he may send the Christ appointed for you, Jesus . . ." (Acts 3:19–20).

The Martyr, Stephen

One of the first deacons in the Church was a man named Stephen. In Acts 6 we read of the appointment by the Apostles of seven men to assist in the ministration of aid to those in need. One of these men was Stephen. He was a person of great spiritual power and boldness. Some members of local synagogues objected to him because he was so forthrightly a Christian. Charging him with blasphemy (sin against God through what a man has said), they brought him to the court of the council for trial. Standing before the council, Stephen, too, preached a sermon. Look at what he said in Acts 7:1–53. See how completely informed Stephen was about the actions of God in relation to Israel across the long years. Doesn't his remembrance of the Patriarchs and Moses remind you of the farewell speech of Moses which we read in Deuteronomy 31, 32, and 33 and of Joshua in Joshua 23 and 24? Enraged by his words, they took him outside the city and stoned him to death. The first time we come upon St. Paul in this narrative is the fact that "a young man named Saul" was present. He consented to Stephen's death (Acts 7:58–8:1). In Chapter 9 we read of that man Saul's conversion on the road to Damascus, the beginning of his great career as Christian missionary and saint.

The persecution that rose after Stephen's death led to the dispersal of the Christians into many places: Samaria, Caesarea, Cyprus, and Antioch in Syria, where the name "Christian" was first used of them.

32

ST. PAUL PROCLAIMS
THE GOOD NEWS

WHEN THE JEWISH CHRISTIANS left Jerusalem to seek refuge elsewhere during the persecution that arose over Stephen, some of them came to Antioch. For the first time on record, these Christians spoke about Jesus Christ to Greeks (Gentiles). "And the hand of the Lord was with them, and a great number that believed turned to the Lord" (Acts 11:21).

Antioch soon became a sort of center for the spread of the Christian Gospel to the Gentile world. It was from there that St. Paul and St. Barnabas started out on their first missionary journey through Cyprus and the central part of Asia Minor. Everywhere they found that the Gentiles were attracted to the message concerning Christ.

Meanwhile Jewish Christian leaders at Jerusalem were highly disturbed over this development of Gentile conversions. The "strict" party at Jerusalem, one of whose leaders was James, the brother of our Lord, insisted that before anyone could be baptized as a Christian, he must first be a Jew, even receiving circumcision, if a male, or special purifications, if a woman.

An Important Meeting at Jerusalem

It was agreed that there should be a meeting of the Apostles and other leaders to consider this whole question. St. Peter, remembering the vision he had had before his visit to the Gentile, Cornelius (see Acts 10), insisted that the Gentiles in

Caesarea had received the Holy Spirit just as much as had the Jews who responded to Christ. St. Paul and St. Barnabas had come up from Antioch to report all that had happened there. It was decided to permit the Gentiles to turn to God— for how could they prevent what was evidently the work of the Holy Spirit! At the same time they decided to send a message to the Gentile Christians urging them to respect the feelings of the Jewish Christians to the extent of not eating meat first offered to idols and keeping other Jewish customs.

More Missionary Travels

We shall not go into detail about St. Paul's missionary journeys, for you can read these for yourself in Acts. Note that St. Paul, accompanied by Silas, went to many cities as far away as Europe. They preached the faith in Macedonia, in Athens, and in Corinth. A third journey took Paul to Ephesus, where the Church was laid on strong foundations.

When St. Paul came back to Jerusalem, he was bitterly attacked by Jewish opponents. Arrested, he was put into prison by the Romans. Because he was a Roman citizen, he had the right to appeal to Caesar. After two years' imprisonment at Caesarea he was shipped to Rome for trial. Read the exciting story of the shipwreck, in Acts 27, and his experiences on the island of Malta in Chapter 28. After three months on Malta, where he made many friends for Christ, his trip toward Rome continued.

"And so we came to Rome" (Acts 28:14). In Rome he made contact with the local Christians and with Jewish leaders, whom he tried to convince "about Jesus both from the law of Moses and from the prophets. And some were convinced by what he said, while others disbelieved" (Acts 28:23–24). The final recorded word from St. Paul we have is his quoting to them from the prophet Isaiah, "You shall indeed hear but never understand" (Acts 28:26). He said that since they would not heed, "this salvation of God has been sent to the Gentiles; they will listen" (Acts 28:28).

The reader feels a certain disappointment that St. Luke does not complete the story. It's almost as if this is going to be continued in the next installment. We never learn what happened to St. Paul. Maybe he *did* intend to finish the story in Part III, but that's only a guess, and probably we shall never know.

Acts and the Letters

One value of Acts is that, by following the story there, we are able to follow St. Paul's travels and fit his various writings into the over-all picture.

The letters (often called *Epistles,* an older English word meaning the same thing) of St. Paul are the oldest writings in the New Testament. As we have seen, he did his writing of these letters before any of the four gospels was composed in its present form. These letters were written out of the very practical desire St. Paul had to keep in touch with the churches which he had founded or visited. The letters were highly esteemed because they came from a beloved leader whom all respected.

To illustrate how reading Acts will help in understanding the letters, let's take a look at Galatians. Chapters 13 and 14 of Acts give details about St. Paul's and St. Barnabas' missionary tour. The people whom they visited on that tour were in the towns and cities of Galatia. They had been well received by many, but many others in the synagogues had stirred up dissension against them because of their work with the Gentiles. Apparently after St. Paul had visited these churches of Galatia, word was being spread about that he was not a true Apostle. He defends his preaching in vigorous words:

> For I would have you know, brethren, that the gospel which
> was preached by me is not man's gospel. For I did not receive
> it from man, nor was I taught it, but it came through a reve-
> lation of Jesus Christ (Galatians 1:11–12).

St. Paul argues against those who have been saying that
the Law is the only pathway which leads to salvation. He
recognizes the Law as having the value of giving the people
a guide until Christ came. He calls the Law "our custodian."

> But now that faith has come, we are no longer under a cus-
> todian; for in Christ Jesus you are all sons of God, through
> faith. For as many of you as were baptized into Christ have
> put on Christ. There is neither Jew nor Greek, there is nei-
> ther slave nor free, there is neither male nor female; for you
> are all one in Christ Jesus. And if you are Christ's, then you
> are Abraham's offspring, heirs according to promise (Gala-
> tians 3:25–29).

St. Paul, in other words, is encouraging the Church people of Galatia to remember that Christ has called them into
freedom from the restrictions of a religion that is based on a
set of laws. He warned them, however, that this does not
mean they shall be loose or immoral. Through love they
are called in Christ to "be servants of one another. For the
whole law is fulfilled in one word, 'You shall love your neigh-
bor as yourself' " (Galatians 5:13–14). He makes a long list
of "works of the flesh" which the Christian is called on to
avoid, including impurity, idolatry, enmity, strife, jealousy,
selfishness, party spirit, and drunkenness.

> I warn you, as I warned you before, that those who do such
> things shall not inherit the kingdom of God. But the fruit of
> the Spirit is love, joy, peace, patience, kindness, goodness,
> faithfulness, gentleness, self-control; against such there is no
> law (Galatians 5:21–23).

Before we leave Galatians, let us call attention to the typical letter form of St. Paul's writings. Note how he starts in 1:1–2, mentioning his name and the people to whom he is writing. Then he gives a blessing in the greeting in 1:3–5: "Grace to you and peace from God the Father and our Lord Jesus Christ. . . ." At the end is another blessing, a kind of "complimentary close," in 6:18. So we start and close letters even today, though much more simply!

33

LIFE IN A FIRST–CENTURY CHURCH

BY READING ST. PAUL's letters we get many glimpses into the life of typical congregations of the Early Church. The reason is that St. Paul is dealing with actual situations and practical problems which the people in the various Christian groups were facing. Sometimes he gives advice; sometimes he scolds; sometimes he praises; sometimes he gives comfort.

Take the Christians at Corinth, for example. To them St. Paul wrote two letters.

St. Paul and Corinth

St. Paul had quite a bit of contact with the city of Corinth when one considers how difficult travel was in the ancient world.

He started the Church in Corinth during his second missionary journey, about which we read in Acts 18:1–18. Apparently he stayed there for about two years. From Corinth he went back to Ephesus for three years. During that period he wrote a letter to the Corinthians which we do not have, but which he himself mentions in I Corinthians 5:9: "I wrote to you in my letter. . . ." He had warned them against certain immoral practices. To this the Corinthians replied, asking St. Paul's advice about various problems in their church. Our I Corinthians is his reply to that request.

St. Paul seems to have gone personally to Corinth when the situation seemed to be getting no better. Not mentioned in Acts, this visit seems to be suggested by II Corinthians

13:1ff. Later he wrote another letter to them, a part of which might be included in the present II Corinthians, Chapters 10–13. Later Titus wrote that things were improving. He decided on another visit and from Macedonia wrote another letter to them which is II Corinthians, at least Chapters 1–9. Then St. Paul arrived for his third visit to Corinth, during which time he wrote the letter to the Romans.

All of this is mentioned to show how cleverly the scholars are able to reconstruct the career of St. Paul, although of necessity much of it must be guesswork based on available facts. He was indeed a busy man, going for visits, writing letters, visiting again, writing some more! All of this shows his great concern for the development of the Church of Christ. We must remember that he was not employed by a promoting agency or a missionary extension society—all of this was largely on his own responsibility, and he even earned his expenses, at least in part, by taking part-time work en route.

The Christians and the City

All of us know how much of our life is determined by the atmosphere in which we live. Every human being is subject to the same kinds of temptations and pressures wherever he happens to live, but the particular form and color these take will be determined largely by the community. Sin is the same in rural Vermont or metropolitan Chicago, but the ways such sin shows itself will vary. In a rural place some forms of troubles young people get into may be due to boredom and the need to drum up excitement. On the other hand, in cities the youth's troubles may be more due to having too many exciting temptations available on every side.

Corinth was a very sophisticated city. It was the capital of the Roman province Achaia, an important trading center between East and West and a busy seaport. People had come there from many places, and the population was quite mixed, though there were more Greeks than any other nationality. Those who know about sports among the ancient Greeks will have heard of the Isthmian Games; these were held in Corinth. There were many religious cults flourishing in the city.

St. Paul came to Corinth in an effort to get the Church started there, to win followers to Christ. It was not the easiest task in the world, considering that the Corinthians were inclined to be more worldly-wise than people in many other places he had visited. In fact, their very situation did prove to be the source of some of the more difficult problems they were to face in the years immediately ahead.

Some of these problems were taken up by St. Paul in I Corinthians.

Problems in Corinth

Here were some of the problems that St. Paul took up about which we can read in this letter.

(1) Party strife (Chapters 1:10 to 4:21). There was quarrelling among various groups of people within the Church.

> What I mean is that each one of you says, "I belong to Paul," or "I belong to Apollos," or "I belong to Cephas," or "I belong to Christ" (I Corinthians 1:12).

St. Paul urges that all remember that they belong only to Christ. "Do you not know that you are God's temple and that God's Spirit dwells in you?" (I Corinthians 3:16).

(2) Immorality (Chapters 5:1–13, 6:12–20). He condemns such practices as incest and prostitution. St. Paul holds up a very high standard for personal conduct and purity of action. "Do you not know that your body is a temple of the Holy Spirit within you, which you have from God?" (I Corinthians 6:19).

(3) Lawsuits (Chapter 6:1–11). It is St. Paul's opinion that Christians should not take disputes to the civil courts, but that they should seek to have these disputes settled within the Church. "Can it be that there is no man among you wise enough to decide between members of the brotherhood, but brother goes to law against brother, and that before unbelievers?" (I Corinthians 6:5–6).

(4) Marriage (Chapter 7). What did St. Paul think about marriage for Christians? He gives his advice: remaining unmarried is good, but those who are called to marry should remain faithful to each other in the marriage relationship. Divorced persons should not remarry. Widows may remarry, but they should marry Christian husbands.

Many other problems are taken up by St. Paul in I and II Corinthians, all of them dealing with very live issues faced among the people. Sometimes his answers are not the exact answers we would arrive at today, but the important thing is that he urged the people to solve all their problems as Christians. There always is a Christian solution for *any* problem.

Romans

One of the greatest letters in the New Testament—and one of the most difficult—is that to the Romans. St. Paul had always wanted to visit the Christians at Rome and now at last was definitely planning to go there en route to Spain. This letter was in a sense a way to prepare the Romans for his coming. The Church had been in existence in Rome for some time already, and he wanted the Christians there to know his thoughts in order that they would support his hoped-for further missionary work in the West.

This is one of the most theological letters of St. Paul's. He takes up such important matters as the meaning of God's righteousness, and the meaning of human justification. How does man "get right" with God, against whom man has sinned? His answer is that we can be justified only through faith and not through any works we can do:

> Therefore, since we are justified by faith, we have peace with God through our Lord Jesus Christ. . . . More than that, we rejoice in our sufferings, knowing that suffering produces endurance, and endurance produces character, and character produces hope, and hope does not disappoint us, because God's love has been poured into our hearts through the Holy Spirit which has been given to us (Romans 5:1–5).

The eighth chapter of Romans is one of the high points of the letter. This has inspired some of the greatest theologians of the Church to some of their deepest thoughts. It is a section you will want to think about and re-read many times throughout your life. It ends on this great note:

> For I am sure that neither death, nor life, nor angels, nor principalities, nor things present, nor things to come, nor powers, nor height, nor depth, nor anything else in all creation, will be able to separate us from the love of God in Christ Jesus our Lord (Romans 8:38–39).

34

"DEAR FRIENDS"

SOMETIMES ST. PAUL had to write his letters under most difficult circumstances. The letter to the Philippians was written from prison, in probably A.D. 62 or 63. It is thought that the Roman imprisonment was the setting because in Chapter 1:13 he referred to the fact that "it has become known throughout the whole praetorian guard and to all the rest that my imprisonment is for Christ"; and in his concluding remarks he sent greetings from "the saints . . . especially those of Caesar's household" (Philippians 4:22). The 4:22 passage suggests that there must have been some Christians who were staff members of Caesar's court—in what capacity we would have no way of telling.

The Church at Philippi

St. Paul's letter to the Philippians has been called "a love letter," in the sense that in it he is telling them how much they have meant to him. The people of the Church at Philippi had sent him gifts of money while he was working in other places. Even when they were unable to send gifts, he knew that they were thinking of him and praying for the success of his labors for Christ. Apparently there had been times when it was not easy to make ends meet. St. Paul writes:

Not that I complain of want; for I have learned, in whatever state I am, to be content. I know how to be abased, and I know how to abound; in any and all circumstances I have

171

learned the secret of facing plenty and hunger, abundance and want. I can do all things in him who strenthens me (Philippians 4:11–13).

Not only had they sent gifts, they also had sent a person, one Epaphroditus, to bring another gift and to stay with him to care for any needs he might have. The messenger Epaphroditus unfortunately got sick and wanted to go back home to Philippi. St. Paul sends him home and sends the letter with him.

Perhaps it is exactly because he is on such brotherly terms with the Philippians that he can also discuss very frankly some of the things in their Church life together that caused him worry and concern. Apparently they have been showing some selfishness and pride. There are pressures on them to give in to the Jewish party within the Church who were saying, as elsewhere, that the Law must first be accepted before one could be a Christian. Some of them may have been thinking that to be freed from the Law gave them permission to behave as those who have their "minds set on earthly things," whose "god is the belly" (Philippians 3:19).

For all these problems the answer is fidelity to Jesus Christ, having His mind in them. "Only let your manner of life be worthy of the gospel of Christ" (Philippians 1:27). "Have this mind among yourselves, which you have in Christ Jesus" (Philippians 2:5).

St. Paul's life with his fellow Christians and his genuine concern for individuals within the Church is brought out in a number of his letters. He mentions by name a number of people who, except for his reference to them, would be completely unknown to history. This shows that the first Christians had a very warm fellowship with one another, and the mutual welfare of one another was their constant concern. In Philippians this concern could extend even to individuals who apparently needed to be told to forget some dispute and "agree in the Lord." He mentions in Chapter 4:2 the names of two women, Euodia and Syntyche, and asks that they be helped, "for they have labored side by side with me in the gospel together with Clement and the rest of my fellow workers, whose names are in the book of life."

Philemon

St. Paul's concern for persons comes out especially in the little letter to Philemon which consists of one chapter of twenty-five verses. This you will have no trouble at all in reading in one very short sitting!

The letter from St. Paul is about a runaway slave named Onesimus. This slave had taken some money from the house of his master, Philemon, in the city of Colossae. He had wandered around the Mediterranean region and finally found his way to Rome. In some way he came into contact with St. Paul, who at this time was a prisoner. St. Paul had known the slave's master, and now he grew to know the slave. Through the Apostle, Onesimus was converted to Christ. St. Paul came to think highly of the man, whom he then called "a beloved brother" and wished that he might keep him nearby in Rome. He thought he should send Onesimus back to Colossae, however, so that he could be restored to his master Philemon.

In the letter St. Paul pleads with Philemon to receive Onesimus back with forgiveness and love. He apparently did not hesitate to urge this, for he knows that Philemon is a Christian who will understand this plea: "Confident of your obedience, I write to you, knowing that you will do even more than I say" (Philemon 21).

Slavery was existent in the time of the Early Church. Sometimes people, looking at slavery from the standpoint of a day when it is seen to have been an evil, say: "Why didn't St. Paul condemn the whole institution of slavery?" That had to come as a work to be done in much later centuries. What St. Paul *did* do was to suggest, in this little letter to Philemon, that even masters and slaves must live with each other in a spirit of Christian love.

35

ADVICE FOR A YOUNG CHURCH

IN ADDITION to the letters of St. Paul which we have discussed
in the last chapters, there are other letters by him in our New
Testament: I and II Thessalonians and Colossians. The letter
to the Ephesians is also attributed to St. Paul in the title and
tradition, although some scholars think it was written by a
follower of Paul's after his death.

Timothy and Titus

There are several other books in the New Testament which
are associated with St. Paul's name, but which seem to have
been written after his death in order to show what St. Paul's
attitude would be toward certain problems that had arisen
later. These are sometimes called the "Pastoral Epistles" because they deal mostly with counsel concerning government
of the Church, the work of the pastors, and so on.

Timothy, to whom two of the letters are addressed, I and
II Timothy, was won to the Christian faith by St. Paul at a
place called Lystra. On his second missionary journey, St.
Paul met Timothy again and learned that he had become
greatly respected as a leader in the churches of the region.
St. Paul decided to invite Timothy to go with him, and from
this time on Timothy appears often with the Apostles. Titus
was a Gentile Christian whom St. Paul also won to the
Church. We know practically nothing about him in detail,
but he seems to have been asked to serve in Crete, where,
tradition states, he became the bishop.

These Pastoral Epistles throw a great deal of light on the life of the Church in the second century. In addition to this value for our understanding of history, they contain valuable advice which is still useful for leaders of the Christian Church.

Among the interesting things we learn from I Timothy is something about the place of women in the worshipping community, the qualities that a bishop should have, and the desirable characteristics of deacons. We learn what was expected of good priests in their pastoral relations to people of many types: old people, widows, teachers, the wealthy, and slaves.

The reference to bishops in I Timothy 3:1–7 is used as the Epistle for Holy Communion in "The Form of Ordaining or Consecrating a Bishop" in the Book of Common Prayer, p. 549; and I Timothy 3:8–13 is used as the Epistle in "The Form and Manner of Making Deacons," p. 530.

When the Church member today reads or hears the admonition concerning bishops, he cannot help but be impressed with the fact that this old New Testament passage is still regarded as saying what needs to be said about the "chief pastors" of the Church:

> The saying is sure: If anyone aspires to the office of bishop, he desires a noble task. Now a bishop must be above reproach, married only once, temperate, sensible, dignified, hospitable, an apt teacher, no drunkard, not violent but gentle, not quarrelsome, and no lover of money. He must manage his own household well, keeping his children submissive and respectful in every way; for if a man does not know how to manage his own household, how can he care for God's church? He must not be a recent convert, or he may be puffed up with conceit and fall into the condemnation of the devil; moreover he must be well thought of by outsiders, or he may fall into reproach and the snare of the devil (I Timothy 3:1–7).

Timothy is urged not to be ashamed of the fact that he is young. This has often been read by young people, who take courage from the fact that the Scriptures say that young people have a very real witness to make for the faith: "Let no one despise your youth, but set the believers an example in speech and conduct, in love, in faith, in purity" (I Timothy 4:12).

Young people also will appreciate the comparisons with the athlete and with the soldier given in II Timothy 2:1–7:

> You then, my son, be strong in the grace that is in Christ Jesus, and what you have have heard from me before many witnesses entrust to faithful men who will be able to teach others also. Take your share of suffering as a good soldier of Christ Jesus. No soldier on service gets entangled in civilian pursuits, since his aim is to satisfy the one who enlisted him. An athlete is not crowned unless he competes according to the rules. It is the hard-working farmer who ought to have the first share of the crops. Think over what I say, for the Lord will grant you understanding in everything.

The reader gets the impression that II Timothy was written by an older man who yearns that the work which he has been carrying on will be entrusted to his competent and faithful young successor.

I Timothy 3:16 contains some words which the scholars think represent one of the oldest confessions of faith and also a very old Christian hymn:

> He was manifested in the flesh,
> vindicated in the Spirit,
>   seen by angels,
> preached among the nations,
> believed on in the world,
>   taken up in glory.

Titus is given counsel on how to lead the Church in Crete. The author is eager to have "sound doctrine" taught (Titus 2:1). He wants to have authority recognized (3:1) and encourages his readers "to live sober, upright, and godly lives" (2:12).

36

"BE DOERS OF THE WORD"

HAVE YOU EVER THOUGHT about the real meaning of the word "sincerity"? It may come from two Latin words, *sine* and *cera*, which, put together, mean *without wax*. In ancient Roman times sculptors would sometimes scratch in those words on their works. Why? Because some unscrupulous sculptors would sometimes chip off pieces of marble in the making of statues with the result that they had imperfect works to offer the public. They would fill in the chipped places with wax in order to deceive the purchasers. An honest craftsman would not want that to be thought of his work. Taken over into our modern language and thought, "sincere" therefore means a person who is genuine, bona fide, one whose actions coincide with his beliefs, one who can be trusted to live as he believes.

The book of James is interested in sincere religion. In one sense the author was somewhat like an Old Testament prophet. He disliked sham, deceit, falseness in any form. In this letter he set forth his goal for the Christian:

> Be ye doers of the word, and not hearers only, deceiving yourselves. For if any one is a hearer of the word and not a doer, he is like a man who observes his natural face in a mirror; for he observes himself and goes away and at once forgets what he was like. But he who looks into the perfect law, the law of liberty, and perseveres, being no hearer that forgets but a doer that acts, he shall be blessed in his doing" (James 1:22-25).

The sincere man will be the opposite of what James called "a double-minded man, unstable in all his ways" (James 1:8; see also 4:8).

The writing is filled with counsel regarding the spiritual life. It is a kind of sermon designed to help people live religiously. It has been pointed out that in some ways the epistle of James is like Proverbs. It even contains various pithy statements which could be called proverbs. Here are a few examples:

> Let the lowly brother boast in his exaltation, and the rich in his humiliation, because like the flower of the grass he will pass away (James 1:9–10).

> The tongue is a little member and boasts of great things. How great a forest is set ablaze by a small fire! (James 3:5).

> The harvest of righteousness is sown in peace by those who make peace (James 3:18).

> The prayer of a righteous man has great power in its effects (James 5:16).

Sometimes people like to contrast St. Paul's emphasis on salvation through faith with the book of James which says: "What does it profit, my brethren, if a man says he has faith but has not works? Can his faith save him?" (James 2:14). James does not deny faith, but simply insists that a man of faith will show his faith in the way he lives. With that there is no disagreement in St. Paul, either, for in many places the letters of Paul give rather complete instructions for living with one another in the Church and in the world. James says "For as the body apart from the spirit is dead, so faith apart from works is dead" (James 2:26).

"The Lord's Brother"

In several places in the New Testament we read about "James, the Lord's brother." (See I Corinthians 15:7; Galatians 1:19; Acts 15:13.) He was regarded in the Church as one of the upright pillars of the new faith. He was killed in A.D. 62. James was one of the strict Jerusalem party who put a great emphasis on the necessity to keep the Law though, as we have seen, at the Jerusalem conference he was very willing to admit Gentiles as long as they were respectful of the feelings of the Jewish Christians.

Traditionally this letter of James has been thought to have been written by the James referred to above. Most scholars doubt that it could have been he who was the author, however. The Greek is of an excellent quality, better than that which a Jewish Aramaic-speaking Christian like James would probably have used. It is widely held by scholars that the letter was written late in the first century by someone whose name we do not know.

More than any other writing in the New Testament, this letter is concerned with Christian conduct. If we took it by itself without seeing it in relation to the gospels and St. Paul's letters, it might seem little different from writings of the Jewish rabbis of the same period, but it is a part of the whole New Testament and with the other writings gives us important counsel for the way in which we should live as Christians.

37

OUR GREAT HIGH PRIEST

SEVERAL TIMES during the course of this book we have mentioned the close relation that exists between the Old and New Testaments. This is evident from the way in which the gospels interpret Jesus as the Messiah. It is shown in the way St. Paul referred to the Christian Church as "the New Israel."

There is one writing in the New Testament which uses symbolism from the Old Testament in a very forceful way to carry out its purpose. This is the Letter to the Hebrews. The King James Version entitles this writing "The Epistle of St. Paul the Apostle to the Hebrews." Scholars are agreed, however, that this is certainly not a writing by St. Paul.

It was written to Christians who were lapsing from their faith. Often when a movement is fresh and new, everyone involved in it is flushed with excitement and busy in it from morning to night. As the enthusiasm wears off a bit, there is a tendency to lose interest and maybe even to go back to ways as they were before. It was this that may have happened to some Christians to whom this author is writing. Were they perhaps Jewish Christians who were thinking of going back to the religious beliefs and practices they had known before they were baptized? This writing was produced probably between A.D. 80 and A.D. 95.

What the writer does is to draw a comparison between the faith of Israel and the faith in Christ. Rather, he shows how Christ is the fulfillment of all that was good and divinely appointed in Israel. He uses the method called allegory—finding spiritual meanings hidden in the words of Scripture.

The book begins by affirming who Jesus is in relation to the Jewish past:

> In many and various ways God spoke of old to our fathers by the prophets; but in these last days he has spoken to us by a Son, whom he appointed the heir of all things, through whom also he created the world. He reflects the glory of God and bears the very stamp of his nature, upholding the universe by his word of power (Hebrews 1:1–3).

In developing his thought, the writer says that Christ was sent by God and was superior to angels and to Moses. Then he refers to Christ as "a great high priest who has passed through the heavens, Jesus, the Son of God" (Hebrews 4:14). The sense in which Jesus Christ is the "great high priest" is that He has identified Himself with us in our human weakness and has taken our sins upon Himself.

The true high priest must be one who can offer to God a sacrifice that will be acceptable to God. Only He who is without sin, and yet who is like us, can do that for us. This is what Christ has done.

The author seems to recognize that he is dealing with an idea that is not too easy to grasp, for he says at one point: "Now the point in what we are saying is this . . ." (Hebrews 8:1). Let that be a comfort if you, too, find Hebrews rather difficult reading. It is a book that you will want to come back to later if you cannot fully grasp it now. Surely this idea of Christ as our true high priest who has entered the very place of sacrifice for mankind is one that we shall more fully understand as week by week we come to God's house and share in the remembrance of Christ's sacrifice in the Holy Communion. The priest says:

> All glory be to thee, Almighty God, our heavenly Father, for that thou, of thy tender mercy, didst give thine only Son Jesus Christ to suffer death upon the Cross for our redemp-

tion; who made there (by his one oblation of himself once offered) a full, perfect, and sufficient sacrifice, oblation, and satisfaction, for the sins of the whole world . . . (The Book of Common Prayer, p. 80).

That is surely an echo of what the author of the letter to the Hebrews, too, is telling us.

38

GOD IS LOVE

IF HEBREWS seems difficult, the two letters named I and II John will, by comparison, seem much easier to read. Do not let their shortness and their simplicity deceive you, however. They, too, deal with the greatest theme about which anyone can write: the love of God which comes to us in Jesus Christ.

Actually, there are three letters named John, the third being called III John. You will note that they follow one another in the way they are placed in our Bible. The third one is a kind of "thank-you letter," addressed to someone in Asia Minor named Gaius. After a personal greeting, the writer expresses his thanks for the hospitality Gaius had shown to some Christian missionaries or preachers who had visited his area. He also makes a complaint about a man named Diotrephes who, unlike Gaius, is not willing to welcome the strangers, even finding ways to get others to refuse to welcome them also.

Christian Fellowship

I John was written to combat what was considered to be a wrong way of thinking about Chirst. Some argued that Jesus of Nazareth was not so important as the spiritual Christ. They denied that Christ had come to earth in the form of human flesh. The people who believed this were called Gnostics. This word means "possessors of knowledge." The Gnostic teachers claimed that they had the secret of true union with

God and said that they were part of a fellowship that was superior to that the Christians had in the Church.

I John says: "I write this to you about those who would deceive you" (I John 2:26). He wanted them to know just what the nature of the true Christian fellowship was.

In the fellowship of the Church we walk in the light, live according to the truth, and are faithful in walking in the same way that Christ walked.

> See what love the Father has given us, that we should be called children of God; and so we are. The reason why the world does not know us is that it did not know him. Beloved, we are God's children now; it does not yet appear what we shall be . . . (I John 3:1–2).

How shall we know that we are children of God? His answer is simple and yet profound:

> Every one who believes that Jesus is the Christ is a child of God, and every one who loves the parent loves the child. By this we know that we love the children of God, when we love God and obey his commandments . . . And his commandments are not burdensome. For whatever is born of God overcomes the world; and this is the victory that overcomes the world, our faith (I John 5:1–4).

Love One Another

The little letter II John has only thirteen verses, two less than III John. It repeats somewhat the basic idea of I John. The author makes it clear that the new commandment is only the one that we have had from the beginning—"that we love one another" (II John 5). He warns against the men who say Christ did not come in the flesh but only seemed to have human form. He warns that these heretics should not be welcomed. Does this deny the sharing of love? The writer seems to be sure, at least, that Christian love cannot really be known except among those who acknowledge Christ. He seems to want to shut the door only on those who come seeking to destroy the fellowship that is known within the Church. They, too, would be welcome to share in *that* fellowship.

The Elder

The writer is said to be an "elder" (II John 1, III John 1). We do not know exactly who the elder might be. It looks, though, as if these three short letters were written by the author of the fourth gospel which bears the same name, John.

39

"KING OF KINGS AND
LORD OF LORDS"

NEAR THE END of the first century an Emperor named Domitian ruled Rome. He was a dictator-king who wanted to have absolute obedience to his rule from everyone in the empire. One of the tests of obedience was the acknowledgment of the Emperor's divinity. This the Christians were unwilling to do since only God was divine and their complete and first loyalty was to Him through Jesus Christ.

Those who have visited the Coliseum in Rome have seen that great stadium where Christians were often thrown into the arena to be eaten by wild beasts while thousands of spectators were entertained. In times of persecution like that, the beliefs and faith of a people are put to a great test.

We know that not all Christians remained loyal to Christ. Some were willing to throw a pinch of incense before the Emperor's statue, even though they may have done it only with tongue in cheek. The really devout Christians were not willing even to think of denying their Lord in that kind of insincere action.

You will recall that the book of Daniel was written in a time of difficulty for the Jews. It was in the form of an "apocalypse," which was an attempt to set down in very symbolical language certain events that were believed about to come to pass. The writer of the book called the Revelation to John, the last book in the New Testament, produced such a writing, probably during the persecution under Domitian.

The writer is designated as a man named John. He wrote from a remote island called Patmos, to which he had been sent when he refused to surrender his loyalty to Christ. As he meditated on his island, he had certain visions which he wrote about in glowing images. He thought of the Roman Empire as the great enemy of God which was about to destroy the Church. He "saw" certain things happening as the visions unfolded.

Admittedly this is difficult reading, for we do not always know the meaning of the symbols which he used. Some of them are clear: the sacrificial lamb, the mystic number seven, Satan, heavenly beings (which remind one of the prophet Ezekiel's writing). Others are beyond our power to grasp. The writing as a whole is dramatic, mysterious, and powerful, pointing to God's final power over Satan and all his works.

At the end, all things are made new by God:

> Then I saw a new heaven and a new earth; for the first heaven and the first earth had passed away, and the sea was no more. And I saw the holy city, new Jerusalem, coming down out of heaven from God, prepared as a bride adorned for her husband; and I heard a great voice from the throne saying, "Behold, the dwelling of God is with men. He will dwell with them, and they shall be his people, and God himself will be with them; he will wipe away every tear from their eyes, and death shall be no more, neither shall there be mourning nor crying nor pain any more, for the former things have passed away" (Revelation 21:1-4).

Another great word to the people of the Church in time of persecution is given in I Peter. There the Christians were even called upon to rejoice in their sufferings "in so far as you share Christ's sufferings" (I Peter 4:13). The theme of I Peter, like the Revelation to John, is: "To him be the dominion for ever and ever" (I Peter 5:11).

II Peter and Jude are concerned with another problem—

false teachers who had risen up in the Church. Jude ends with a wonderful benediction, which will be a good place for us to end, also:

Now to him who is able to keep you from falling and to present you without blemish before the presence of his glory with rejoicing, to the only God, our Savior through Jesus Christ our Lord be glory, majesty, dominion, and authority, before all time and now and for ever. Amen. (Jude 24).